The (Mis)Adventures of Pete North, an Ordinary Working Lad

Pete North

The (Mis)Adventures of Pete North,
an Ordinary Working Lad

Copyright ©2020

Pete North has asserted his right under the Copyright Designs and Patents Act 1988 to be identified as the w author of this work.

A CIP catalogue record for this book is available from the British Library.

This book is sold subject to the condition that it shall not by way of trade or otherwise be lent, resold, hired out or otherwise circulated without the publisher's prior consent in any form of binding or cover, other than that in which it is published and without a similar condition, including this condition being imposed on the subsequent purchaser.

I have written this story for my beautiful wife, Shirley,
my three wonderful sons, Ryan, Aaron and Brandon,
my cute granddaughter, Renée, and all of my descendants
yet to bless us with their appearance.

CONTENTS

Introduction
1. Family Background and Childhood   1
2. Apprenticeship   13
3. South Africa   19
4. Zambia   37
5. Return to England   63
6. Back to Zambia   73
7. Sierra Leone   97
8. BB&S   149
9. America   191
Conclusion, Written by Shirley   245

INTRODUCTION

I had so many extraordinary experiences and adventures during my time in Africa and America from 1963 to 1983. On 12th October 2020, I reached the age of 80. As I approached this milestone, I felt it was time to write down my stories and share them with you.

From the age of 15, I wanted to travel and do something different with my life. Here in my story you will read of my escapades: my encounters with witchcraft, life-threatening situations, hitmen, adversity and corruption, plus stories about escaping jail, making many friends and much more.

During the writing of this book, I have relived every episode in my head and heart. It has been like having therapy: reliving emotions and releasing some of the pent-up feelings with which I have lived for the past several decades.

These stories are of my recollections and are not intended to inflict blame or upset.

Enjoy!

CHAPTER ONE
Family Background and Childhood

My full name is Pete Maxwell North. My mother wanted to call me Carl, but as we were at war with Germany, Carl seemed like a German name, so they settled for Pete. My father's name was Joseph North; my mother's name was Kathleen Paul.

My maternal grandfather had died in 1939, the year before I was born, at the age of 45. I was told that it was due to injuries from when he had been gassed in the First World War. There is a picture showing him in his wheelchair.

My paternal grandfather was called John Robinson North (born 1884), and his wife was Annie McCartney (born 1880). My paternal grandma in Huddersfield was only about four feet tall. In fact, she had to put a stool in front of the sink and stand on it so that she could reach to do the washing up. However, she ruled that house, make no mistake about that! She only had sight in one eye because, as a child, she had been hit in the eye with a stone. Her bad eye was permanently closed.

Together, my paternal grandparents had seven children, three girls and four boys, of which my father was one. People had big families in those days; going back through earlier generations, people were having up to 12 children. Some of the names were unusual. For a while, I thought we had a naval admiral in the family. It turned out my dad actually had an uncle whose given Christian name was Admiral (known to the family as Addy). There was also a Marsh North, a Carter North and a Collinwood North.

My grandparents lived in Almondbury, a suburb of Huddersfield, and I remember visiting them there when I was a child. We would often go on a Sunday, when all the families would gather, including all my cousins. The adults would play cards, and the children would join in. It was quite good fun. Some of my cousins were a lot older than me, but there were a couple who were close to the same age. I was not as close to them as they were to each other, because I did not live in Huddersfield past the age of four years old, moving to Earby and then Accrington.

My grandfather used to work on a big golf course in Huddersfield, Woodsome Hall. He was responsible for cutting the grass there, and my father would go and help him, which was how my dad became interested in golf himself. When they were cutting the grass on the greens, they had to cover the horse's hooves with rags so that they would not dig in. They did not have tractors or modern types of lawnmower back then when my dad was a small boy, so the grass cutting equipment was horse-drawn. My grandfather even helped build the stables where the horses were kept. My grandfather did a bit of everything workwise really. He used to tell me stories of how, at one time, a job he had was to transport furniture to the new boarding houses that were just opening up in Blackpool. Huddersfield to Blackpool is quite a long way, 80-odd miles as the crow flies, and he would walk the whole distance, leading the horse, which was pulling a cart filled with furniture. It would take a week or so to get there and similar to get back each time he made the trip.

I had a sister, Christine, who was four years older than me (born 1936) and who unfortunately died about four years ago. I also have a half-sister called Ann, from a later relationship of my father's, so she is a lot younger than me. We are still in touch, and she lives in Huddersfield.

I was born in Cowley in Oxfordshire on 12th October 1940, during the Second World War. My dad was a toolmaker and was working in the Morris factories on tanks and aeroplanes, including Spitfires.

He was deferred from the army because of his skills. Toolmaking was the most highly rated skill in engineering and still is today, I believe.

While we were in Oxfordshire, my dad used to go around all the gyms just to spar and practise. One day, he was in a gym, and there was a man, a manager, looking for someone to box against his client, who turned out to be Bryn Williams, an up-and-coming young boxer who was unbeaten. Without knowing who he was beforehand, my dad volunteered to box him straight away. They started sparring, and my dad could see a weakness, so he hit him and flattened him! The manager was going crazy! Bryn had long unbeaten runs in his career and even fought for the British Championship, although he never won it. My dad should have taken up boxing as his career, but, unfortunately, he broke his thumb while working one day, and that ended his boxing and other sports. There was no pay if you were off work in those days.

My dad also played golf and table tennis. I played a lot of table tennis during my apprenticeship, but I could never beat my dad. When he was 70 years old, my dad played golf with a local team in Huddersfield. He beat Bobby Locke, who was the world's number two player! The guy went mad! Bobby Locke was that good that he had been banned from playing in America, because he kept winning all their tournaments. The guy won everything. For some reason, he must have come to Woodsome Hall Golf Club in Huddersfield, which was where my grandfather had looked after the greens. I have no idea why he ended up there that day, but they partnered him with my dad. I think Bobby was about 66 at the time, and he died just a few years later. They used to say that after a few drinks Bobby would pull out a ukulele and would get everybody singing. His drinking might have been a problem that led to his relatively early death. After they had played, my dad would get people walking up to him in the street to shake his hand, saying, "You're the guy who beat Bobby Locke!"

My mum and I left Oxfordshire when I was about 18 months old and went back to Huddersfield, where both my parents originally came from. In my early years, I can remember the blackouts and the bombed-out buildings. Huddersfield was not particularly badly hit, but, like all places, it still did have some bomb damage.

The house was a back-to-back, so we only had a front door, and the tippler toilet was down the yard. In the toilet, there was screwed up newspaper in place of toilet paper, and we had a tin bath in the house. Upstairs, there was only really one room, which we partitioned off. There was a gas range in the scullery.

As the war was finishing, when I was four years old, we moved to a little village called Earby. My father went to work for Rolls-Royce in Barnoldswick, a nearby small town in the West Riding of Yorkshire. We lived in a prefab bungalow, which was made of asbestos, but it also had a toilet, a bath and two bedrooms. My sister and I shared one of the bedrooms. My mum stippled the walls with a potato dipped in paint. One strong memory from that time is that my dad used to make me stand up at the table to eat. He said it was good for the digestion, but it was only me whom he would not let sit down. Maybe it was because we didn't have enough chairs!

We were not wealthy, but we always had enough food, and, in a way, we were in luxury living in the prefab, because we had an inside toilet. I had to lay the fire when I got home from school each day, starting by raking out the coals, adding tightly wrapped up newspapers, then some fresh coal and then lighting it. The fire heated the house itself and also our water.

I started school in Kelbrook, a small village near Earby, and I can remember that we had to carry gas masks with us. I had to go over the fields to get to the school, which was roughly two miles away. I walked alone; my mum did not accompany me, as she was working, and my sister was older and attended another school. One day, when I was about six years old, I was on my way home and decided to climb a tree. I then decided to jump out of the tree, but, on the way down, a branch caught on my short trousers and I fell awkwardly, breaking my arm. The doctor came to the house and said, "This is going to hurt for a minute." He just sat next to me on the couch and pulled at my arm to realign the bone. I then went to the hospital in Burnley, where they put my arm in plaster. They must have taken an X-ray while I was there and thought something was not right. They then had to break and reset my arm again. The good old days!

My dad had passed the examination to go to grammar

school at 9 years old, 10 years old and 11 years old, but his parents could not afford to buy him the uniform needed for grammar school, so he never went. He was very clever. Unfortunately, I did not have my dad's brains when it came to school; I was not that academically clever, especially when it came to spelling. Today, I often still cannot remember how words are spelt and have to ask Shirley! My primary school was just a normal small country school. I can remember that there were beds where they would let us take a nap in the middle of every school day. I was good at making models out of plasticine and generally enjoyed school, although I remember being told off for making noise and sparks with the clogs I wore.

My father started his own business in Earby with a partner. It was a sheet-metalwork and engineering company, and he did well at it. It grew to be quite a decent sized concern. My mother worked in the cotton mills at this time, which was noisy work with long hours. When I came home from school, she would still be at work, so that was when I would begin to light the fire.

My dad was only about five feet six and slim, but he could bend and break six-inch nails. He was incredibly strong. He loved playing football. Once, when they were courting, my mum went to watch him play. She had to walk miles to get to the game and arrived there late. By the time Mum had arrived, Dad was on the touchline.

She said, "I thought you were playing?"

He replied sheepishly, "I was, but I was sent off."

Dad was frequently sent off due to 'sorting out' the opponent's tough guys! For other players, he was the man to go to if they were being given a hard time by one of the opposition players. My dad would swap positions with them and tackle hard.

My dad also played cricket and opened the batting for the local team when he was just 12 years old. When we lived in Earby, he would play cricket with the local team and would regularly score 50s! He could do anything. His hand-eye coordination must have been fantastic.

My parents split up when I was 10 years old. My mother and I went from Earby to Huddersfield for about six months, where we lived with my mother's sister. Then I was taken by my mother to live in Accrington, a small town between Blackburn and Burnley. My older sister, Christine, stayed with our father, and I only saw her occasionally from then on. Unfortunately, Christine then contracted tuberculosis and ended up in a sanatorium. She lost part of a lung to the disease. I believe she never forgave my mother for leaving her. I tried and tried umpteen times to get her to come and meet my mum, but Christine would never agree, and she never spoke to my mum again. She was very hurt. My mum remarried later on, but her second husband subsequently died of a heart attack. He was a nice guy, but I was overseas by then, so we were not especially close.

When my mother and I moved to Accrington, we initially stayed in digs, where we just had a front room, and I slept on a bed in the bathroom. My mother had very little income. Then we ended up in a council house in a suburb called Huncoat. The story goes that it got its name when a troop of soldiers was passing on a very hot day and the sergeant said, "OK guys, uncoat!" There were stocks in the village, which I believe are still there today. The house had a nice back garden where I could play football. We had a coke stove in the kitchen to heat the water. We had no carpets upstairs, but it was comfortable enough. My mother got a job with a company called Masterbar, which made equipment for the mining industry. She was a machinist and worked long hours, including Saturday mornings and two late weeknights overtime.

By the time I started at school in Accrington, I had missed the 11 plus, but I would not have passed anyway! I went to Hyndburn Park Secondary School, which was fine, and I had nice friends there. I became very good friends with a lad who lived nearby and who was cock of the school, so I had no problems with bullying or anything like that. The school was quite a distance from our house, and I had an old bone-shaker bike for a while, which I used to get there. My mum did not like it, but all mums worry, don't they? I became house captain at school and was a prefect in my third year, which was unusual, because they usually only picked people from the fourth year. I always liked history and was goalkeeper in the school football team. I also liked cricket. Accrington was in the Lancashire League, and, from the age of 13 or 14, I would walk down to the cricket field to watch matches and practise. I used to have to walk along the wall that ran down the side of the railway. I was in their under-18s team when I was 14. My form teacher, Mr Harrison, played cricket for Accrington at that time. I think he was a PT teacher, and I got on well with him.

Mr Harrison had a slipper with which he used to hit pupils as punishment, while the headmaster, Mr Davidson, had a strap. Everyone called Mr Davidson 'Diddy' – don't ask me why. It was embarrassing to be called out in front of the entire school at assembly and be strapped for some wrongdoing. Other teachers had the cane, but the funniest one was the woodwork teacher, who had a big T-square. He used to put a chalk mark on the T-square and then whack you till he could see the mark on your trousers. As children, we learnt respect and did not answer back. I did not get into that much trouble, although I did experience the cane, slipper, T-square and strap in my time.

My maternal grandfather

My paternal grandfather and grandmother; note her size,
as Grandad was only - at most - five feet six inches

Uncle George, my mum's brother-in-law, and me. He was home on leave, 1942

CHAPTER TWO
Apprenticeship

I had to leave school at Christmas, as I had turned 15 years old in the October. Our football team had never been beaten in that final year, but, because I left, I did not get to see out the end of the season. There were no exams for me to sit before leaving, as this was back in 1955, when I had just turned 15 years old. After leaving school, I tried to get a job. There was somebody in the school whose role it was to ask students what they wanted to do, a sort of careers advisor, and then somebody told me there was a job going in a repair garage in Green Haworth, which is right up on the hills, away from anywhere. I went there and got a job for which I was paid 15 shillings a week. It was the worst job I have ever had in my life. I was trying to repair cars, but generally I just got covered in oil all the time. The guy with whom I was working did not want me there in the first place. Then it so happened that the boss knew someone whose son wanted to be a mechanic, so I was asked to leave. I was only there for a few months. I was just a gopher, it was terrible and I did not like it, so I was not upset to leave.

I then managed to get an interview for an apprenticeship with a massive engineering company called Langbridge

Ltd in Accrington. They were the second biggest in the Accrington area. They had a huge fabrication shop, as well as large shops for machining, fitting, turning, moulding, sheet metal, maintenance, patterns and woodwork. The foreman's cabin was up some iron steps. I went up there for my interview. I wanted to be a fitter but was told that there were no vacancies left for fitters. The only vacancy left was for a plater, so he asked me if I wanted to be a plater. I answered that I did not even know what a plater was! He pointed down to the shop floor and said, "You see those things down there, one of the lads who was 18 made them." I remember thinking that would do for me. That was it: I was successful at the interview, and I became a plater. A plater is involved in making anything out of steel, be it sheet steel, angle iron, girders or anything else fabricated out of steel.

I was paid £3 5s a week, which was brilliant. I split the wage with my mum. I worked from 8am to 5pm each day. I would also usually work on a Saturday morning, and most weeks I would also get two late nights overtime as well, when I worked until 7pm. I worked alongside different qualified engineers to learn from them. Everybody has different ideas on how to do things, so it is good to learn from a mix of people. It was a very busy company. There were a lot of coal mines in the area, and Langbridge was doing a lot of work for that industry, fabricating large-scale equipment and so on.

We had a canteen, and the best thing I remember was the big thick slices of toast I could get there. We also had potbellied stoves in the middle of the fabrication shop. We could get two welding rods and bend them into forks, stick our sandwiches on the prongs and then toast our sandwiches in front of the stove – that was brilliant! The company had its own football and cricket teams, and I was lucky to get onto both straight away.

One project I worked on as an apprentice was a massive construction which was built to go over the train tracks and fill the coal trucks as the train passed underneath. It consisted of two massive round hoppers, tapered towards the bottom, either side of the control cabin, which was sat high above the tracks. One particular day, I was up on top of the cabin, putting the roof on it. Lots of holes had been drilled, but they never lined up with one another. To do the job, you would have to knock a podger, a metal bar, through to align the holes. Then, when the man on top of the roof shouted, the guy inside the cabin would tap the podger with a hammer so that it would jump up out of the hole. The man on top could then stick a bolt through, and the other guy underneath could stick a nut on it. On this occasion, I did not have time to shout, and when the guy below hit the podger, it flew up into the air and I missed catching it. It fell way down to the ground below, where there was a guy sitting with no hard hat on. It hit him, and he staggered about, with blood everywhere. He had a big dent in his forehead after that. Nothing was ever said to me about it; accidents happened a lot, and there was no such thing as health and safety back then. There were furnaces for riveting, and the men used to throw and catch red-hot rivets.

During the apprenticeship, I also went to day school to learn other skills; a sheet metal qualification was quite an involved process. The apprenticeship lasted five years, so I completed it when I was 21 years old. I just missed being called up for national service, which stopped just a few months before I finished serving my time. I stayed with Langbridge for a short while after I qualified. They put us on piece work then, and every job was timed. I used to run about, trying to get this cut and that welded. Other blokes would just be standing there, much more relaxed. I could not understand how they were then able to go and log that they had saved 10 hours on a particular job, when I was running around trying to save one hour. It was not until later that I twigged that they were managing it just through having much more experience. They could plan a job and use their time much more efficiently. This was a learning curve for me.

While I was an apprentice, I went on a couple of holidays during the summer shutdown period. One was to Butlin's in Pwllheli, and the other was to the Isle of Man for a week with seven or eight other apprentices. We had a great time, with lots of drinking, obviously. Back in my teenage years in Accrington, I think I was lucky to grow up at the time of the birth of rock 'n' roll and Liverpool beat music, led by The Beatles and The Stones etc. Alas, I was to leave at the height of it to fly off to South Africa.

I was still living with my mother at this time, and she was still fit and working hard too. By the time I reached 22, I was starting to wonder if this was me now for the rest of my life. I knew one of the lads in the office, who was marrying one of the girls from the office. The factories had streets running off them, and they had bought a house in a nearby street. Their new house was next door to the girl's mother, who also worked in the company canteen. Was that what I had to look forward to? I knew it was not for me. Just around then, one of the older guys, who was in his 30s, told me he had applied for assisted passage to South Africa. Australia and South Africa were looking for people to go and work there. I thought Australia was a very long way, but South Africa was a bit closer. I wrote to South Africa House and was soon given a ticket at the cost of £10. I do not think my mother was especially happy about me leaving, but I could not stay where I was. I was only in touch with my dad very rarely at that point in time, so I did not discuss it with him either.

I got myself a passport and then got my dad to take me down to London. He dropped me off at the house of my friend, Andy, who was living in St Albans. I had a night out with Andy, then, the next day, I went to the airport to fly from Heathrow to Johannesburg. I can remember that my bags were way over the weight limit, so I ended up in the airport giving a load of my clothes to Andy. I even had to give him my leather jacket, which broke my heart! One part of the flight was particularly scary when we went over the Congo and the plane dropped thousands of feet in turbulence. The trolleys had just been around serving breakfast, and the uneaten breakfasts went everywhere! There was a little child sitting next to me whom I was trying to keep from crying, when all the while I was shit scared myself! This was around 1963, when the aircraft was a turboprop not a jet. At the end of a long journey, which included stops for refuelling, I finally arrived in Johannesburg.

CHAPTER THREE
South Africa

When I got off the plane in Johannesburg, I then had to catch a train to Cape Town. The journey was about 1,000mi., and it took a long time. I got off at one of the stations to try to get something to eat. It was just a tiny little station, and I soon found that everything was shut. Suddenly, the train started pulling out, so I had to run and jump back on before I was left behind. When I reached Cape Town, I was blinded by the sunlight. It was around Christmastime, which is summer there, and the temperature was around 100°F.

I had the address for the Amalgamated Society of Boilermakers, of which I was a member and which represented all the trades associated with metalworking. I went straight there when I arrived in Cape Town. The man there gave me details of digs where I could stay for the first week. He told me to relax for a week, enjoy the town, then come back the following Friday, when he would find me a job. The digs, a sort of mini hotel, was a flea pit, and I was covered in bites in no time, but, during the day, when I explored, I found Cape Town to be a lovely place. It was strange to be somewhere that I did not know anybody, just wandering around. It was 1963, I was 23 years old, and all I had brought with me was my suitcase and £60 I had made by selling my car, a Ford Consul, before I left England. The Consul had not been my first car. Before that, I'd had a van, a Ford 8, which had cost me £7 and which I had sold for £10! When it was raining and I drove uphill, the wipers stopped working!

During that first week, I managed to find myself some new digs to the north of Cape Town, out towards Table Mountain. It was just one room with a shared bathroom across the hall. It was not much of an improvement, as I could not lock the door. I did start to wonder what I was doing there. Throughout Africa, there was always a slight feeling of having to look over my shoulder, of never feeling totally relaxed about safety. Apartheid was ongoing at this time, and I would work alongside black lads who were employed as labourers or helpers. They were not treated in any way badly by us, or by the Afrikaners – that I saw – however, I did see bad treatment going on in town. The worst to me seemed to be the police. I was once sitting in a cafe when a black African lad ran in. The police followed him and started beating him with batons. It was terrible.

Cape Town was an eye opener to a small-town lad. Mind you, the nightlife in Lancashire was just taking off at that time. Groups were springing up everywhere, every pub seemed to have a band or a group, and it was the start of the cabaret clubs. In Cape Town, there was no nightlife as such. It was also hard for me to find friends, apart from apprentices from where I worked.

I had told the man at the union that I would like to work in shipbuilding; to me, that would be the pinnacle of my career. When I went back to see him the following week, he took me to a company called Globe Engineering, and they did repairs to ships. They had one branch inland and one on the docks. The following Monday, I started at the inland factory, although I was later moved to the docks. This experience was a real awakening for me. It was a big company, with lots of equipment that I had never even seen before. At Langbridge, if I had wanted a piece of steel, I'd had to use a straight-line burner to cut it. At Globe, they had guillotines, powered rollers, press brakes, all sorts. Things I had never seen nor heard of before. Every time I was given a job to do, I had to go and get one of the apprentices and say, "I am sorry, but the machines I am used to were nothing like this; how does this one work?" That was how I got through the work, and I got away with it!

Another problem was that the Afrikaners would not speak English, so if I spoke to them, they would just ignore me. I quickly realised they hated us. It all stemmed from the Boer War, when thousands of women and children had died in concentration camps from starvation, disease and illness. In due course, I became friendly with a German guy, who said, "You want to learn a bit of Afrikaans." He told me that the language was similar to German, and he taught me a few different words. From then on, any time I was near a group and heard them yakking away in Afrikaans, I would just throw the odd word in. It surprised them, and they started speaking to me in English, because they did not know how much Afrikaans I knew and whether I could understand them. That broke the ice and helped my situation.

Unfortunately, the foreman was a bastard. He would stand in his doorway with his arms folded and shout people's names. The people he called would immediately run, saying, "Yes, sir." I remember thinking I was an

Englishman; we do not do that, so I would just walk to him instead. There was one job though that I was nervous about being given to do, and I knew at some point the foreman would assign me to it because he obviously didn't like me as I wouldn't put up with his bullshit and call him 'sir'. It was when they cut out the side of a ship that was wearing thin or had been damaged. It would be roughly 10–12ft wide by 20–30ft long and either concave or convex (curved both ways). Every time one of these jobs came in, I kept a close eye on how it was done. Sure enough, my turn came, and it was a big, roughly burned-out shape, curved both ways. The first job was to make a cradle bent to the shape out of a half-inch square bar. I then had to bend each piece to the shape, tack weld them together and make it fit the cut-out piece. It had to fit like a glove. The second job was to find a sheet of steel thick enough and big enough. Using an overhead crane, I had to get the sheet under a massive steam hammer (similar to what a blacksmith would use) and then work it under the hammer to get the concave shape in the plate in the right places. This could take a week or more to get the exact shape, and I would need to keep trying the cradle until the shape was identical. The last job was to put the cut-out shape onto the new sheet and then, using the old shape as a template, burn it exactly to the rough shape. When the job was done, it was then sent back to the docks to be welded into place.

Finally, I was sent to work in the docks, which was great. I enjoyed the fresh air, sun and wind, although my nose used to peel at least once a fortnight. They had the biggest dry dock in the southern hemisphere, half a mile long, and hell it was deep and wide. We had a flagship tanker in at one time, and it filled it. When you were up on the decks, it was massive and a long way down straight to the dockside floor. God knows how they work on these super cruise ships nowadays. One of the best jobs was having to sail out to sea on trials on boats I had worked on. From there I could see the sun come up and light up Cape Town in the very distance.

I began to adapt to life in South Africa more and more. While I was working on the docks for Globe Engineering, two Geordie lads arrived. They were platers like me and had been working on the shipyards of the northeast. They lasted two days in Cape Town before they said, "This is not like home; we're going back!" and off they went! I thought it was important to stick it out and see what came of it. I would write a letter home once a week, that was all the communication we could have in those days, and my family would write back to me.

I found South Africa to be a bit like the UK had been 20 years earlier. It seemed old fashioned in some ways; for example, young people would still be chaperoned. I was once invited to church, and it was so boring that I fell asleep, plus the service was in Afrikaans. I was never invited again! I used to go to the bioscope cinema. There was one called The Tearoom Bioscope where, when you bought a ticket, you also got a cup of tea and a biscuit!

One of the apprentices I had met working inland for Globe was in a music band. At one time, he wanted me to become their manager. I told him I did not know anything about music management and turned the job down, but I did advise him that if they wanted to sing Beatles songs and other 1960s pop music, they would have to lose their Afrikaner accents. I would meet up with them and have a few beers now and again.

While I was in Cape Town, I played football. The first team I played with was Cape Town City, a semi-pro team. They had five goalkeepers already, but I did manage to get on the bench as a substitute. They had a nice stadium and had joined up with a Greek team, Helenica, and they would alternate training and Saturday matches between the two teams. At my tallest, I was five feet nine and a half, while all the Afrikaners were at least six feet! Back in England, I was average height, but I put my comparative shortness down to lack of nutrition. I was born during the Second World War, and my parents were born at the time of the First World War. By comparison, the Afrikaners had had a much better diet, with fruit and everything else. One of the other guys, a goalkeeper, had even just come back from playing professionally for Charlton Athletic. Cape Town City was a club made up of professional or semi-professionals. I was certainly never paid anything by them, and I never got a game, so I did not stay long.

I then found out there was an England football set-up, which played on Sundays. In Cape Town, absolutely everything was shut on a Sunday, but somehow this international football league played on that day. England had three teams in the leagues, and I went straight into the second team. There were teams from all over the world: Ireland, Scotland, Wales, France, Germany, Austria, Switzerland, Italy, Greece and others I have forgotten. The England first team had a goalkeeper, but their second team did not, and I started playing in goal for them. We started winning every game and were running away with the league on an unbeaten run. The third team was doing the same even without a regular keeper. The first team also wasn't doing badly and was winning most of their games.

Unfortunately, at around this time, I ended up getting yellow jaundice as a result of infectious hepatitis. I do not know for definite how I got it, but I suspect it might have been through the scrapes I would regularly get diving for balls as a goalkeeper. The ground was very hard, and although the pitches were grass, the surface was very rough. I had only been in South Africa for a few months, and I was off work for two weeks before anyone found me, laid up in my digs and very ill. An insurance man called, and when I answered and invited him in, he called an ambulance for me. I did not realise until later how serious it was. I was taken to Groote Schuur Hospital and was in there for a month. After about three weeks, the people from whom I had rented my digs came to see me. They told me they wanted some money for rent, and when I told them I had no money to give them, they made me write a letter to Globe Engineering, demanding that they give my wages to my landlord – how bad was that? Even worse, Globe gave them the money. At that moment, I decided that, as soon as I was recovered, I was leaving those digs and finding somewhere else to stay.

I was on a medical ward with some other men, most of whom I became quite friendly with when I was finally able to get up and move about. When I explained my situation, one of these guys said, "Come to my house; my wife has a boarding house." He gave me the address, and, when I was discharged, I just went to my old digs, put all of my belongings in my car (a Simca Ariane) and left. That car was the worst one I have ever had in my life; it was a jinx. One night, Friday 13th would you believe, I had a date with a girl. After we left the cinema, I went to unlock the car door, and the key snapped in the lock. Everything went wrong with that car! Another time, it broke down on Adderley Street, the main street in Cape Town. The accelerator cable had snapped. This policeman came running over telling me I could not stop there. Of course, I said that I was sorry and explained what the problem was. I told him to let me go into the big store (which I was next to) to get some string. I got the string, managed to join the cable together and drove off red-faced!

I arrived at the boarding house, which was in a suburb called Observatory, and knocked on the door. The man from the ward was still in hospital, but I had seen his wife once or twice when she had been visiting. I told her that her husband had said I could stay there, and she replied that they had no room. I said, "I am not going anywhere else," and in the end she found me a room in the backyard. The property was just like a terraced house in England, but bigger and with a bigger yard at the back. I was in a small room at the side, with just enough space for a bed and somewhere to hang my clothes. I also got meals included, and she made up lunch packs for me as well – what a bonus!

I came back there one night in the dark and put the light on in my room only to see a big spider on the wall. It was a king baboon spider, which is part of the tarantula family, and it is massive. Argh! Whilst I was staring at it, wondering what to do, its legs started to flex like it was going to jump on me. I took my shoe off and splatted it against the wall; all the legs were sticking out the side of the shoe! What a job it was to scrape it off my shoe. I slept with the light on for about two weeks after that!

The man I had met in hospital eventually came home, but I did not see much of him around the boarding house. He was an alcoholic who drank wine all the time and had been in hospital because of cirrhosis.

Based in one of the houses which backed onto the boarding house was a taxi firm. The owner of the taxi company had a baboon, and it was evil. The owner had used chicken wire to cage off three quarters of his backyard as an enclosure for the baboon (poor thing). Baboons are not daft, they are quite clever in fact, and this rascal made several holes in the fence to enable him to put his hands through at will. One of the African women who came to do the washing was walking past one day when the baboon got its hand through and grabbed hold of her wraparound robe and pulled it off her! Whoosh – no dress! Soon after, a chicken wandered past. Before you could say Jack Robinson, the baboon grabbed it and the hen was inside the pen getting humped to death by one happy baboon! When the owner was cleaning out the cage, he would chain the baboon to a big pole out in the large area at the back of the houses. Local dogs would gather and bark at the baboon, and it would run around and chase them. The baboon would then shorten the chain bit by bit. When he had enough slack, he would release it and pounce on one of the dogs – end of dog!

As I have mentioned, my Simca Ariane always caused me a lot of trouble. On one occasion, the carburettor was not working properly, so I took it off to have a look. I stripped it in two halves, and then I did not know what to do. I decided to go and ask at the taxi office, as I had often seen them fixing cars at the side of the road. I forgot all about the baboon that I would have to pass on my way there. I was walking through the yard with the carburettor in both hands when suddenly the baboon reached out and grabbed me by the hair. It started banging my head on the fence. All

I could do was hit its hands with both bits of the carburettor until it let go. When it finally did, it had two big tufts of hair in its hands, and I had two big bald spots. When I looked round, the baboon was there looking through my hair for something to eat – the swine!

I believe that the baboon eventually escaped and climbed up onto the roofs of the buildings, where the police had to shoot it.

As I was recovering from my illness and starting back at work, I found where the next England football match was going to be, and I went along. When the guys saw me, they went crazy, and then they gave me the money which they had been collecting for me every week, unbeknown to me. I was penniless, and they handed me about £50 (wages were about £18 a week). How kind of them! I was still too ill to play at that stage. A couple of weeks later, it was coming towards the end of the season. The first team was in the final of the cup, whereas the second team had been losing their games since I had left. The third team was also on a winning streak and was in the final too, but they still had no regular goalkeeper. The third team then asked me if I would come and play for them in the cup final. I agreed, and it was a brilliant experience.

All three finals, for the first, second and third teams, would be held on the same night at Cape Town City's ground, under floodlights. We were on first and playing the Greeks. Our captain looked around and said, "I have only seen one of those Greek players before; we have never played against any of the others." They were from the Hellenic team. They had put all the semi-pros in for the cup final in place of their usual players! We held them to a 0-0 draw. I thought there would then be penalties but was told that no, it was over at that, perhaps due to the time constraints of playing all three games in one night. I was just happy that I had not let them down, as I was still weak.

The team in the second league then came on for their cup final, followed by the first team, who were playing Scotland. The rest of the third team and I wanted to go into the dressing room to wish the first team luck, but we were not allowed in.

When it came to the last final, Scotland's first team was led out by a piper. This was a really stirring scene! Now it was England's turn. Out came 11 children dressed in the England's football kit for the kick about. After a poignant pause, out came the England players, each dressed in a bowler hat, coat and carrying a briefcase and an umbrella (just like they would if they were going to work in an office in England). They lined up facing the children and took off their coats and hats and handed them to the children, who marched off with them. It was brilliant! What a plan! Everyone cheered like mad. Back to the game: we lost 3-2, and Scotland, with the piper, won the cup, but what a great night it was. All I got from that night, besides fantastic memories, was a small England pennant!

By this time, I had heard about another company in the dock area which was building a diamond dredger. They were paying a lot more money than I was getting with Globe, and I really needed higher wages, so I went over there and was taken on straight away. It was a great place. They had a big cabin where we could all eat lunch every day. There were people of all different nationalities around this big, long table. The Africans who made tea for us had two big urns; in each they would tip in a packet of tea. One urn would then have a tin of Nestlé sweetened condensed milk added, while the other one remained unsweetened. It was vile! Both were so bad that I could not drink it!

One of the men was an Afrikaner called Van Boom. He had an unfortunate affliction whereby any loud noise would make him jump. Guys would try to scare him on purpose. We used to throw paper balls at him when he was drinking so that his tea would go all over the place. One particular day, the cabin was full and there was no seat free for me to sit on, as I had arrived last, so I was perched on a toolbox in the corner. I finished my sandwiches and scrunched the greaseproof paper in which they had been wrapped (in those days, bread wrappings made a super-tight ball). Without thinking, I threw it in the direction of Van Boom. I did not even take the time to aim it properly. By pure luck, or bad luck, he was just taking a drink when it hit him, and he got such a fright that he jumped up and knocked his tea and sandwiches over. Mistakenly thinking it was the guy across from him who had thrown it, he dived over the table at him! The table was knocked over, and everybody's tea and sandwiches were on the floor. Oh God, what had I done? It was just like something from a film – absolute chaos – but I survived!

When we had finished work on the diamond dredger, we were sent miles inland to a big factory. There I met up again with a guy called Victor, who was from Burnley and had been in the same fleapit digs as me during my first week in South Africa. He was a welder and would entertain the Afrikaners by giving them sermons. The Afrikaners were so religious that they really enjoyed the sermons. Vic was so believable that they were entranced. Vic was also a very good mimic. He could imitate anybody or anything, had an unbelievable memory and would do a whole show for you at the drop of a hat. He could sound exactly like this old general manager I'd had back at Langbridge during my apprenticeship. Victor is still the best mimic I have ever heard. When you talked to him, he would never use his own Burnley accent; instead, he would imitate one of the guys with whom he worked, and you could always tell straight away who it was. Sometimes he would imitate me – the bastard! I met Victor again quite a few years later, and he told me that if ever he was short of money, he would go into a Working Men's Club, get himself up on stage and do an act imitating whatever the top telly or radio shows were at the time.

I quickly got fed up at the inland factory, because there was very little to do, so I left and went back to Globe Engineering. They in turn sent me to Simon's Town naval dockyard, where I worked on South African navy frigates. I was doing similar work to what I had previously done for Globe but on a massive scale, burning huge pieces out of the sides of frigates and then attaching new pieces in their place. One thing I really enjoyed about the work was that, after I had worked on repairing a ship, it would go off for trials, and I would get to go with it. It was beautiful to be out at sea on the ship all night, seeing Table Mountain from a distance. It was a military environment with personnel in uniforms who went through all the rigmarole of piping a captain or some dignitary aboard. This was not on the ships we were working on, but we could see it on other ships. Five or six of us would drive out there together every day. We had a foreman in charge of what we were doing, but he used to wander off during the day. We used to wonder where he was going. On board the frigate that we were working on was an operations room with a periscope. We pulled it down and used it to keep an eye on where the foreman was. When he wandered off, we would down tools for a break! The periscope was brilliant; it had normal vision, wide-angled vision and zoom vision.

Working on the dockside meant that we were subjected to very windy situations most days. It used to take ages to get the knots out of my hair with my fingers every night. By this time, I had the Elvis-style haircut. The winds on the docks were always blowing at 60 or 70mph. As my hair started to get longer, the situation got worse, and I got fed up with it. To heck with it. Out came the scissors, and I cut myself a fringe so that I could see. Bingo – no more worries about my hair. I was the first person in Africa to have the Beatle cut! Mind you, I still have it in that style today, though not as much as I would like.

Back when I was working at Langbridge, it was a colleague there who had first told me about assisted passage. That guy had been headed for Cape Town, so I had decided I would go to Cape Town too so that there would be at least one person in the area whom I knew. As it turned out, I only ever saw him once, because he was living quite a distance away from Cape Town itself! He then got a job in Zambia, working on the copper mines. He used to write me letters saying how beautiful and brilliant it was there and how much money he was making. My wages at Simon's Town were still just around £18 a week, so I decided to apply to go to Zambia too.

During the time I was waiting to hear about my application, Globe sent me back on the docks to work on a large building which they were putting up. As an apprentice, when they were building the Preston bypass, the first motorway, I had been sent out to put the metal handrails on the bridges. I had learnt there how to get them square with a spirit level and to assemble them. I just applied the same method to putting these huge steel columns inside this building at the docks. Quickly I realised that, as I was moving along, putting the columns in, another team was coming along behind me and bricking up in-between them; they certainly did not hang about! I remarked to one of the blokes on site that it was a really big, tall building, and he told me I should ask for 'height money', as it was dangerous work. I asked and was given an increase in my wages: the impressive amount of 1s 9d (approximately 7½p) extra per week! I had just finished this job when I got the nod to go to Zambia.

Building a diamond dredger for South West Africa. On the docks, Cape Town, 1964

My friend, Mr Baboon, in his cage

CHAPTER FOUR
Zambia

By this time, in late 1964, I had changed my car from the jinxed Simca Ariane to a Simca Vedette. It had a small-bore V6 engine and was a good car. I packed all my belongings into the car and got ready to leave. My landlady said she would make me some sandwiches to take with me on my travels. She said, "Pick a chicken, and I'll cook it for you." I picked the biggest one, and then she passed me the axe and said, "Here you go. Kill it." I told her I couldn't, so she did it instead!

I set off on the 2,000-mile journey to Zambia. First, I had to drive from Cape Town to Johannesburg to go to the main office of the mine union. On the way there, the radiator overheated in the car. I managed to get into a little town, where I stayed the night while my car was fixed. When I finally reached Johannesburg, it was late in the afternoon, too late to go to the office. I tried to find digs for the night and was turned away from everywhere I tried. I realised it was because of my long hair, shorts and T-shirt. I had to comb my hair back and put on a proper shirt and jeans. Then I tried again, and they let me in!

The next day, when I spoke to someone at the main office,

they said, "Sorry, you have taken too long, so that job has gone." They said they had a vacancy for me in a town called Luanshya, on the copper belt. I drove over 900mi. from Johannesburg to Luanshya. I got through South Africa with no problems, and then I got to Zimbabwe, which was still called Southern Rhodesia back then. Driving up through there, I found that a lot of the roads were not like roads at all as I knew them. There would just be dirt roads with two clear tarmac strips about 18in. wide for your tyres to follow along. If you met another car coming the other way, you had to move over and pass with just your far-side tyres in one track, and the other driver would do the same on their side. It went on like that for miles and miles. Every time you came to a bend, you had to sound your horn to make sure nobody was coming the other way in the middle of the road. On one occasion, I came round a bend, and there was a snake lying across the road. I could not stop in time and went over it. I got out to look and could see both ends and the middle still swishing about, but I could not see the head nor the tail, as they were still in the bush at either side of the road; it was one massive snake. I quickly decided to get back in the car and get out of there. It must have been a boa constrictor of some kind.

I called in at Bulawayo, which is a beautiful town. The streets are incredibly wide, because formerly a lot of ox wagons would arrive there, so there needed to be space for them to turn around. The name Bulawayo means 'the place of killing', as this was the area of the Matabele tribe, who were an offshoot of Shaka's Zulus, a minor tribe of Zulus who escaped the wrath of Shaka and went north into Southern Rhodesia (now Zimbabwe). The town was built by the settlers to this new country in the days of Cecil Rhodes, after whom the country had been named (Zambia was previously Northern Rhodesia). My impression of Zimbabwe in the 1960s was that the people were superb and very friendly (both black and white). Everywhere I went, they were telling me, "Don't go to Zambia; stay here." Everybody offered to find me work, no problem. I was really tempted, as they were the nicest people I had ever met. However, I was committed to going up to Zambia.

I then stopped off at Wankie Game Reserve (now called Hwange), where I was chased by an elephant! I was driving through the reserve and spotted a group of elephants. I then saw a path off to the side, which I drove down. The elephants were not far away, then all of a sudden one of them started running towards me. I put the car in reverse and sped off as fast as I could. I did not know much about elephants then, but I learnt after!

Before I reached the border with Zambia, I arrived at Victoria Falls. What a place that is. The African name for it is Mosi-oa-tunya, which means 'the smoke that thunders'. The Zambesi river divides the two countries and the falls – wow – they are something else! It was discovered by Dr David Livingstone, the intrepid missionary explorer, in 1855. The falls were described by Lord Curzon as 'the greatest river wonder in the world'. I was driving alongside and went through a rainforest which runs the length of the falls. You have the mist and rain coming across all the time, but it is really hot, so I had both the car windows down. Suddenly, I spotted this beautiful little monkey. I pulled over and took a picture of it. As I took the photograph, another monkey jumped in the window at the other side of the car. Then the first monkey jumped inside the car too. They were grabbing all of my belongings which were packed in the car. I ended up fighting them both! Fortunately, I won, because they would have wrecked the car and everything in it.

I stopped at The Victoria Falls Hotel, which is a beautiful collection of old colonial buildings. The next morning at breakfast, I had never seen a spread like it: they had everything, and it was just marvellous. I tried to eat my way through it, but I did not quite manage the lot! Then I took a trip on the Zambezi, where I was able to see crocodiles and hippos, before I crossed the border and entered Livingstone, which was awful. I was shocked that it was so poor compared with the other side of the river. The buildings were just hovels. One thing that particularly struck me as I was driving these long roads was how little there was to see: just miles and miles of scrubland and forests. In England, you would see a farmhouse or something now and then, but here there was nothing.

I just kept driving and eventually found my way to Luanshya – what a beautiful place! I was going to work at the Roan Antelope Mining Company, and Luanshya is a company town purpose-built because of the mines. The mine was founded by William Collier in 1902. He shot a deer, which landed on the deposit of green malachite (copper ore). The deer was a roan antelope, hence the name. It was the first mine that came into production in 1929. Luanshya is just one of the smaller mining towns that make up the copper belt in Zambia.

What a lovely little town it was. The buildings were all white and the town was nicely laid out. The houses were nice little bungalows with plenty of land for growing all sorts, mainly bananas, mangoes, avocados etc. In the main area, at the main clubhouse, there was a shop, a bar, a cinema, a dance hall and a theatre. Across from there was a large outdoor swimming pool, and next to that was a big mess hall or restaurant, where bachelors such as me got our meals for free for the first week. To the side of the main area was a rugby club, which had the sports fields behind it. There were tennis, bowling, baseball and cricket facilities too. Everything was central, and then the houses were laid out beyond that.

My initial accommodation was set quite a long way back from the main area. It was a building that was split into four units, and I had a bedroom and a bathroom to myself. On the first night, I unpacked my belongings in my room and headed off to get something to eat at the mess. When I got back to my room, I found I had been robbed, cleaned out: my passport, my apprenticeship papers, everything was gone. Whoever had done it had cut through the gauze and broken the window to get in – the bastards! When the police finally arrived, it was like something out of Carry On Constable! They just did not have a clue what they were about. There was this young white clerk whom they had to ask what questions to ask. Luckily, I still had one suitcase which I had not yet unpacked and had just pushed into a corner of the room. The thief had stolen everything I had unpacked but not this closed case. I had to send off for replacement papers but did not recover any of the other belongings that were stolen.

I refused to stay in that accommodation after being robbed, so I was moved to another room that was closer to the main area. There was a row of all bachelors living next to each other, and it was quite good there. During my first week, I was friendly with a couple of guys from Sheffield, Yorkshire. We had all arrived on the same day. They were both male nurses at our hospital. At first, we met every day at lunchtime and then it became more infrequent later on, due to them working shifts. We still had our friendly rivalry, with me coming from Lancashire and them from Yorkshire – 'The Battle of the Roses' (mainly cricket and football). After about six months, I heard the sad news that one of them had committed suicide. It appears that a nurse he had met at work, and to whom he had become engaged, broke it off just days before the wedding. This break-up must have hurt him really badly for him to become suicidal. Being a nurse, he had access to tablets and used them to overdose. I helped carry his coffin at the funeral. It really upset me; how tragic and pointless it all seemed. Why hadn't he spoken to us?

What a great place the camp was, with super weather and lots going on everywhere. There was boating and swimming at a big lake, which was a mile wide and three miles long, and a super clubhouse. I tried water-skiing, but I wasn't very good. The best fun was dinghy sailing, until I needed a wee or got hit with the sail boom. It was magic. Of course, water sports were only for when I was not playing cricket on Saturdays and Sundays. There was a very high standard of teams from all of the copper belt, now and again with the odd ex-county player in the team. Of course, there were also a lot of South African lads who were a class act too. Even the rugby teams had ex-rugby union players in them. We had one lad, John Lacey, who was over seven feet tall and I think had played one game for England. I did not play myself, but the club life was amazing. All the pastimes had a club: tennis, bowling, hockey, horticulture etc. You name it, they had a club for it. That meant that, after work was over for the day, it was a great social life. At the clubs, they would put on snacks and such for us single lads. Free food kept us alive.

We used to start work at 6am and finish at 3pm, so we had lots of time to socialise or do whatever we wanted. It was there that I learnt karate, though only as far as a green belt. Nevertheless, learning various styles of karate and also a few years of kung fu stood me in good stead later in life. In my late 60s, I did some Kaze Arashi Ryu, a style of ju-jitsu based on how the samurai is trained. I was 67 when I started and stopped after a slight heart attack a year or so later.

I made a lot of good friends and good workmates whilst I was in Luanshya. It really was a good life. The money was twice as much if not more than I had ever earnt in my life.

I was quickly given the nickname of Ringo, due to my Beatles-style locks. After being christened in this way, I don't think anybody ever knew my proper name. Mind you, the Africans with whom I worked gave all the white people names. Mine was Pickinin Bwana, which literally means 'young boss'. I was very young compared with my workmates, who were all in their 50s or 60s. The only other nickname I can remember anyone having was Hamba Gash, which is the African name for a chameleon, and the guy they gave the nickname to was in his 60s and moved very slowly, like a chameleon. When I first arrived there, nobody had seen anybody with long hair before. I had last had a haircut back in England! All the mine apprentices had their heads shaved as a ritual, and rumours were out that they would grab me and shave my head. Against my principles, I swallowed my pride and visited the local barbers for a trim (the swines). After that, I let my hair grow again.

The African whom they gave me as a helper/labourer was certainly a few knives short in the cutlery drawer. The Africans were paid monthly, and on the day they got their pay, they would all go down to their local bar and buy two one-gallon jars of local beer (which was white with bits in it). Then they would drink themselves silly. My labourer told me that he was fed up with his wife, so he went and bought a new one, much younger. He said he paid £5 for her. After one of these drinking sessions, he staggered home, and, as he walked into the house, his new wife hit him over the head with an iron skillet. When he recovered, he took her back to where she had come from. I don't think he got his money back!

I was working on an overhead crane track very high up (in a loading bay). I had put the extension ladders up on full extension and was climbing up with one hand full of tools. My boy was supposed to be holding the ladders, because below me was a lot of broken castings. As I was nearing the top, the ladder started sliding away. Luckily, not too far away was an upright structure holding the rails, so I dived full length and managed to grab part of the angle iron frames. Mind you, the rest of my body hit the structure with a bang. I was sore for a week. When I looked down, the labourer was sat across the way. He finally got the ladder back for me to climb down. Boy was I lucky! I refused to work with him again. It caused a big stink, as we had to have at least one boy working with us as part of Zambianisation. I stuck it out for quite a while until I was forced to have one. At least I got to choose one who had worked in a gang when we had a big job to do. I had noticed that he had more sense and personality than the rest. When I went back to Zambia eight or nine years later, the same boy had done really well and was in charge of a machine in the big machine shop. He deserved it!

I played football for the African team Roan Antelope. They had a stadium in their township. They weren't bad, and we used to train once or twice a week and then play on Sunday, either at home or away against other teams on the copper belt. I was playing out as a fullback. One Tuesday, when I arrived at training, everybody was saying, "Where were you on Sunday?" I replied, "Sorry, but my name wasn't on the board on Thursday." They dragged me over to the board and pointed. I still could not see my name. They shouted, "There!" and pointed to a name, Pete Maxwell. When I had signed the form, I had put my full name, Pete Maxwell North, not thinking that they would use the first two names and miss the last. Anyway, it was soon cleared up. I had some good times with the team. One funny story took place when I was playing in a game at home. Being fullback, I was covering the goal, as the keeper came out and missed the ball. I dived and got my hand to stop it from going into the net. The referee must have not seen it through all the players' legs. Anyway, the ball was still bobbing about near the goals and players were rushing in. Being on my hands and knees, I just dived and headed the ball out for a corner. On Monday back at work, I noticed a big crowd of our African workers in a large huddle. In the centre of the crowd was our local comedian, a very funny African. He was telling them his version of what had happened at the match.

"Mr North was on his hands and knees, and he covered the ball with his hair. Nobody knew where it was, they were shouting, 'Where's the ball?'"

Of course, the crowd were all falling about laughing their heads off. He was on his knees, reckoning to cover a ball and wafting hair over it. To see it happening was really funny, and it is hard to put into words how he captured that moment.

A friend and I shared a motorbike, a Triumph 500 in a

Bonneville frame, which we would ride around the camp. Then, disaster struck. Rhodesia had made a Unilateral Declaration of Independence (UDI) in 1965 (later becoming Zimbabwe). The UK prime minister, Harold Wilson, then told Mr Smith, the prime minister of Rhodesia, that he must give everyone the vote, equal for blacks and whites. Mr Smith said he would give the vote to people who reached a certain educational standard, which was simply passing primary school level. It is hard to put into perspective that the majority of the Africans who live in the bush have no education whatsoever. The only ones who had any education were those who lived in or near towns. Most towns in the bush would have schools, mainly run by missionaries. Smith's reasoning was that if they reached that basic level, or higher, of education, then they would understand what they were voting for. It would not be mob rule, which came much later, under Mugabe.

As a result of this disagreement, Wilson organised the embargo, which cut all the lifelines into Rhodesia, including railways and roads. We were cut off. All our goods and food and so on came up from South Africa or Mozambique, into Rhodesia and then up into Zambia. When they closed the borders, we had nothing coming in, and we could not get the copper out; it was a two-way system. They tried to find other ways to get stuff in, including through the Congo and a place up in the north end of Zambia, but everything was knackered. The bridges were down, and they had been left in disarray. Whatever transport lines there were had collapsed. We were snookered. They ended up bringing in some big aeroplanes from America. We were down to a supply of just one gallon of petrol a month.

During the early 1970s, bearing in mind that I was not

there then (I had left in 1966), the Chinese built a railroad in from Mozambique. Zambia had asked Britain if they would build it, and they had taken one look at the terrain and said, "No chance." The Chinese agreed to do it and completed it in around 1972. When the main trainlines arrived in Zambia, they were the wrong gauge – just a nightmare. The stipulation was that Zambia had to buy goods and food from China in return. Then all the people who had worked on this railroad could live there. Squirreled away all over Zambia were these camps of Chinese people and their families. Every month or six weeks, they would come into town on wagons. Hundreds of them, all with the same drab green uniform and hat on. They would empty every shop and then head back into the jungle. Zambia had gone downhill fast.

Back to 1965. As I said, we were rationed to one gallon per month. The mine got organised and provided buses to collect us for work and take us home, but I could see that the writing was on the wall. After five months of this, I had saved five gallons of petrol, and an apprentice friend of mine, Albert, had done the same. I persuaded him to come with me to the Congo, to Elizabethville, now called Lubumbashi. I used to read a lot as a schoolboy and was into all the Tarzan stories and films, which were supposedly based on the Congo. Elizabethville was roughly 200mi. away. His car would do 20mi. to the gallon, while mine would do less. We put our cases into his car and filled it up with the petrol, then put the empty drums in the back.

Instead of driving straight up to the border, past all the towns in the copper belt (about 150mi.), we opted to go to Ndola, about 20-odd miles away, then go another five or six miles into the Congo. It was well known that people had been sneaking into the Congo and buying petrol in the first village. That was our reasoning too and why we brought the empty drums. That turned out to be the biggest nightmare of my life, and we nearly both lost our lives. It cost us bribes to get through customs, and then about 10mi. or so on we came to the turn-off to this village. We turned left and then another left down the village street, which was mud huts and thatched roofs. We stopped outside the place that was supposedly selling petrol. It was a mud hut with the front opened up and propped up with sticks, not like a shop that we would recognise, just sacks and boxes of stuff stacked up against walls. When we pulled up, there were no people about, just the odd one talking to the shopkeeper. He said that, yes, he had petrol, but he was charging twice the price, which seemed a bit much to us, so we tried to barter him down.

The language there is not English but French from the Belgian occupation. The lad who was with me had been born in Zambia and had grown up speaking Chickabanga, which is a universal mine language. Zambia has 72 tribes, each with their own language. This area of the Congo is rich with mining industries from copper to diamonds etc., so they understood the mine language. Whilst Albert was conversing with the men, the store suddenly filled with Africans, as did the street outside. The atmosphere then turned hostile, and I could see what was happening. I whispered to Albert to keep smiling and to tell funny jokes and stories whilst we backed slowly out through the people. Talk about cutting the atmosphere with a knife! By this time, they started shouting and spitting at us. We managed to squeeze into the car, which they were rocking. I told Albert to back out slowly and hope that we didn't run over any toes or people (there were hundreds of them by now). Luckily, we managed to reverse to the top of the road and back to the main road, where we spun around and set off again for Elizabethville.

Whilst he was reversing back out of the village, I noticed quite a few cars which had been stripped out to the shell or burnt out. I got to thinking that we were worth a lot of money to them, with our cases full of clothes, our car and whatever money we had hidden about our person. I realised that we were lucky to get out with our lives. That was scary. Plus, there was the fact that nobody would know where we were or what had happened to us. We would just have disappeared. Just the odd person knew of our plans, but not of our detour. We had just finished work at 3pm on Friday and had jumped in the car and left, knowing that we had to be back to start work again on Monday morning at 6am.

We arrived at Elizabethville by 10pm that night and managed to get a room and a meal: T-bone steaks, the biggest steak I had ever seen! The rest of the trip was also harrowing. All the way up, we were stopped by army patrols. At least four times they wanted bribes. We had hidden packs of cigarettes and money for things like this, and by the fourth time, we had run out, so we were lucky to get through. The next day, we spent all morning calling at petrol stations for fuel. Every one of them refused us, as their country had put a ban on selling petrol to outsiders. By this time, we were getting worried, as our petrol was running low. I took a gamble and suggested that we would go back to the outskirts of the town, as we had noticed a petrol station coming in. We drove out there, and luckily it was owned by a Belgian. He took pity on us, but we had to drive the car into the garage for him to fill the drums. He did so, and we left with both the tank and the drums full. The Belgian was scared that someone would see him if he used the pumps to fill them.

Just a mention of what had happened prior to our visit: rebels had been killing whites on the mines and at the missions, killing and raping the nuns and selling white men's body parts in the markets. There were battles between the rebels and an army backed by mercenaries. Elizabethville was a mess, with most buildings covered in bullet holes. The roads were also full of holes made by mortar fire.

We were glad to leave by Sunday morning. I had bought an elephant tusk from the marketplace on Saturday afternoon, then I realised that we would have to go through the main customs into Zambia. I took the back seat out and wedged it between the springs. The border was only 50mi. from where we were staying, and we chose that way as the safest, 150mi. through the copper belt. Again, there was trouble at the border post, with army everywhere. They stripped the car, opened our cases out on the floor and gave us a really hard time. We were there for about two hours until another car came up behind us, and, right away, they said, "Go!" Then they turned on the other car, which was now going to go through what we had suffered. We threw our stuff into the car and sped off into the sunset.

As I said, we had about 150mi. to go, and when it started to go dark, our lights wouldn't come on. The dynamo had packed in. So long as we didn't stop, we could keep going, but it was difficult to drive in the dark, as the road was surrounded by forests and not much light came from the moon. A car passed us, so we kept following his taillights for about 100mi. When he carried on where we had to turn off for Luanshya, the car started to struggle. My mate manged to get us near to someone he knew, and we went and knocked him up, begging a lift into town where we lived. This was at about 1am. I will never forget that whole adventure until the day I die. All because I read some Tarzan books as a schoolboy!

After that, everything else seemed mundane. I was in a pantomime over Christmas; that was a great experience. I think it was Puss in Boots. They wanted me in a musical called The Boyfriend, which is set in the roaring 1920s. I stuck it for a few weeks in rehearsals, but then I realised I would never be comfortable dancing and performing, so I quit (I don't think they missed me, and it went down quite well). Mind you, I missed all the fun at the bar after the rehearsals!

Northern Rhodesia gained their independence in 1964 and changed the country's name to Zambia. Kenneth Kaunda became the first president, but he used underhanded tactics to persuade various tribes to vote for him and the party. He would send his army and delegates to bully the tribes. One such case was a small independent tribe in the northwest of Zambia who had their own religion called Lumpa. It was a branch of Christianity, run by an old lady called Alice Lenshina. Kaunda sent his delegates to make the tribe vote for him, but Alice and the tribe were not interested and sent them packing. Kaunda then sent troops in with mortars and all the latest armoury. The poor tribe had just what they hunted with: a few bows, spears and arrows. Between 700 and 1,000 people died. The army burnt the villages to the ground and jailed Alice and her husband, and she died still in captivity in 1978. Her beliefs were quite simple: she believed in Christianity and in trying to abolish witchcraft and polygamy. Some of her followers escaped into the Congo and are still there today.

It was a great life for me, but the World Cup was coming up in summer 1966 in England. None of us had radios or televisions in the copper belt. I thought I had better leave and head home. I realised afterwards that I should have taken leave and then come back after the World Cup instead of quitting altogether – another bad mistake!

The journey home was quite an adventure too. I took a train journey back into Rhodesia, then I got another train to Mozambique to head for Beira, the main port. There I would catch a ship home. The train filled up with people going to Beira for Easter. It took five days to get there by train in the end. What a busy place Beira was! Every hotel was booked up (no room at the inn!), but luckily I had met someone from Luanshya who was staying on the beach in a tent. He offered me a very small one-man tent, and I jumped at it. It gave me somewhere to put my case and sleep for a couple of nights until I could board the mail ship. Luckily, at night, they had an area for a disco (the first time I had heard that word) on the beach. A band played good music, and we had a ball.

The ship was amazing (to me) but obviously nothing like the cruise ships of today. That was another month's holiday, as it stopped at every port. One of the main ports was Mombasa for five days. While the boat was docked there, a couple of friends and I hired a car and set out for Tasavo game park in Tanzania. We also made for Mount Kilimanjaro. We managed to get part the way up, but we were on a three-day safari. In the whole three days, we passed only one car going the other way. We saw most animals, including lions, at the side of our road. We were chased again by a large elephant that came out of the bush just in front of us. We must have startled it, as it turned towards us with ears flapping and trunk waving from side to side, making that old Tarzan-type call as it set off running. I did not know that cars could go as fast backwards as forwards! We managed to get out of range from this angry elephant. Some of the lodges that we stopped at were very nice and near waterholes.

Back on the ship, it called at Zanzibar and a small place called Bemba. These were places where the Arab slave traders used to collect slaves. We stopped at Aden, which used to be a main stopping point for ships for oil. We were told not to go beyond three streets from the front, as there was a lot of unrest. Of course, we ventured further, looking for bargains. I bought a new camera and binoculars. We nearly walked into a bunch of rioters carrying a dead body; his hands and feet were tied with a pole slung through. He was being carried by two people. The rioters were screaming and shouting and were hitting him with sticks. We did a sharp about turn and ran back – not a pretty sight! Once again, another big mistake.

The ship's next stop was Egypt. A few of us got off at Suez and got a bus to Cairo. That was a long, horrible journey, with no air conditioning, and it was so hot in the bus it was practically unbearable going through the desert. The only good thing was seeing herds of camels wandering about. We finally booked into the Nile Hilton Hotel, which was nice. The next day we visited the pyramids and then the Cairo museum. I was totally blown away by it all. You were not allowed to photograph the exhibits, but I sneaked a couple of good ones of King Tut – brilliant!

The next big stop was at Naples in Italy, where four of us caught a train out to Pompeii. Again, it was unbelievable. We managed to find a guide who took us to all the places you were not meant to see. The arena was blocked off, but we found a way in. What a magical place. The rows of seats were numbered, and we got into the area where the gladiators and animals were kept. Then we had cheese and wine out in the middle of the arena, sitting on the grass – wow! I took some nice pictures as well. Then we stopped at Gibraltar for a day or so, where I bought my first transistor radio. That was brilliant for catching all the pirate radio boats (such as Caroline) playing all our favourite music. Then it was back to Blighty. It was a shock seeing all the white faces again, because everyone on the ship was so sunburnt!

Passing the Drakensberg mountains. Notice the water bags on the front and sides of the car; the water kept cool due to the wind

Beware of elephants and hippos crossing the road

This is the rascal that tried to chase me

Dr Livingstone, I presume... was the first white man to see the falls and named them after Queen Victoria

What a beautiful sight

As I was taking the picture, another monkey jumped
through the window, causing havoc

Facts about the Falls....

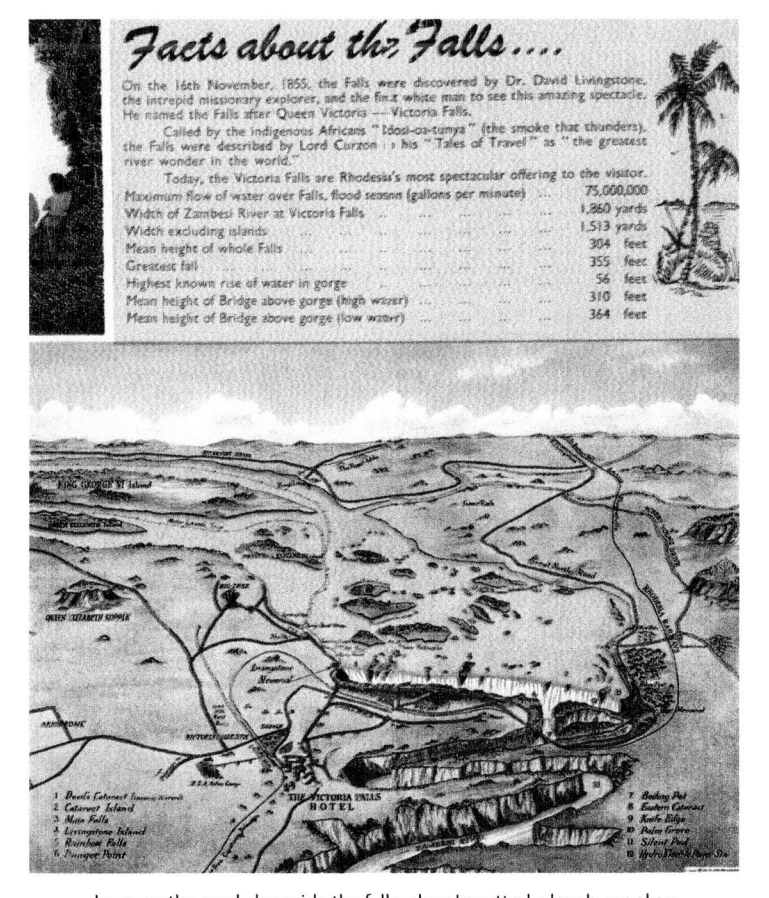

On the 16th November, 1855, the Falls were discovered by Dr. David Livingstone, the intrepid missionary explorer, and the first white man to see this amazing spectacle. He named the Falls after Queen Victoria — Victoria Falls.

Called by the indigenous Africans "Idosi-oa-tunya" (the smoke that thunders), the Falls were described by Lord Curzon in his "Tales of Travel" as "the greatest river wonder in the world."

Today, the Victoria Falls are Rhodesia's most spectacular offering to the visitor.

Maximum flow of water over Falls, flood season (gallons per minute)	75,000,000
Width of Zambesi River at Victoria Falls	1,860 yards
Width excluding islands	1,513 yards
Mean height of whole Falls	304 feet
Greatest fall	355 feet
Highest known rise of water in gorge	56 feet
Mean height of Bridge above gorge (high water)	310 feet
Mean height of Bridge above gorge (low water)	364 feet

1. Devil's Cataract
2. Cataract Island
3. Main Falls
4. Livingstone Island
5. Rainbow Falls
6. Danger Point
7. Boiling Pot
8. Eastern Cataract
9. Knife Edge
10. Palm Grove
11. Silent Pool
12. Hydro Electric Power Sta.

I was on the road alongside the falls when I spotted a lovely monkey

How white everything was in Luanshya

This is the concentrator where I worked on the Roan Antelope Mine

These are some of the guys I worked with in the concentrator

Repairing the ball mill in the concentrator

One of the houses I looked after when the owners were on holiday

Ringo - that's me - on the bike I used to ride around the sites

"Ringo"

Don't spend it all at once

All the best

From "The Boys"

When I left Zambia, they gave me a cheque, among other leaving presents

On the journey home, I stopped off in Egypt and sneaked a picture of King Tut

CHAPTER FIVE
Return to England

It was May 1966 when I arrived back in England, on a Friday night, with the Cup Final due to be played the following afternoon. That was a bonus for me. Everton beat Sheffield Wednesday 3-2. I was living with my mother again, but, of course, although she had got a telly by then, it was only a small black-and-white one. I then received a phone call from my dad saying, "Please come and work for me." He had his own business in Earby, a small backstreet engineering company. His earlier partnership, Bell Metal Industries, had split into two smaller companies doing different types of work. My dad's side was called West Craven Engineering. Working for my dad was always interesting workwise because of the nature of the different types of work that we handled. My dad was a slavedriver. He would not let us wash our hands until it had gone 12pm, whereas I was used to washing my hands well before lunchbreak started, ready to eat. All he would do was just have a drink of tea then take his cup over to one of the lathes and carry on working during his lunchbreak, never stopping. I really learnt a lot from him, such as how to manage my time more productively. All this came to fruition later on in life.

As I have said, my dad's business partner was a sheet metal worker, so he concentrated on that side of the business, and my dad concentrated on the engineering side. I fitted in well with that, doing welding and things like that.

As I mentioned earlier, I had done a year's study of karate in Zambia. In the mid 1960s, karate was not popular at all; in fact, nobody really knew about it apart from those who had been in Japan during the war. I learnt it from a guy who worked with me in the mine and who used to meet with the Japanese trawlers who came into port when he lived in South Africa (that was where he had learnt karate). I had earnt a green belt. One particular day, I was working with my dad in a mill. My dad had left the keys in his car so that if it was in anybody's way, they could move it. It had been pouring down with rain that day, and when we came back to the car later, we saw that it was stuck in a massive ankle-deep puddle. A wagon driver saw our situation and was bragging away and calling my dad names. My dad opened the door of the wagon and dragged him out. He was going to beat the hell out of him. I dragged my dad off, got the car out and told him to drive back to our work. About an hour or two later, it was dinnertime, and as I walked back to our place of work, I could see just one car sitting in a car park opposite.

My dad said, "That guy has been after trouble with us. I told him you were a karate expert and would go and sort him out."

I went out, and there were five blokes in this car. I said to them, "Everybody out. Let's sort it out!" I recognised the one who was driving as a guy I had seen a week or two before at a summer fete; he was a strongman! I just took the mickey out of the guy my dad had been arguing with, telling him to pick on somebody his own size, and, in the end, they just chickened out and drove off. Thank God they did, because that weightlifter would have killed me!

I started to play football and cricket again. One of the football teams I joined was in one of the local leagues around Accrington. Believe it or not, the team was called Cambridge Street Methodists. It was run by David Lloyd's dad. David Lloyd is a cricket commentator on Sky TV and was a professional cricketer. When we played together in the football team, I was about 25 going on 26, and he was only about 19 years old. When I had left England in 1963, David had just broken into the Accrington first team in the Lancashire league as a slow left-hand bowler. He was very young, just about 16. By the time I came back from Africa, he was playing for Lancashire and ended up as opening batsman for them. He went on to play for England and scored over 200 runs in one game. After he had finished playing, he became an umpire in the main leagues and was then coach for England for a while before he became a commentator. David was also a good footballer and played in his dad's team. He'd had trials for Burnley and could have chosen to play for them, but instead he chose cricket.

In one particular football match we played in together, a cup semi-final, he was our number 10 (inside left in those days) while I was in goal. At half-time we were drawing 2-2. In our huddle, David said, "Don't worry, lads. If it's still 2-2 near the end, I'll get us a penalty." One of our opposition's defenders was a part-time wrestler. Not very tall, but he was tough and hot-headed. In the last five minutes, David went in and charged on their goalkeeper as he was gathering the ball. It used to be rough on keepers in those days. You could only take four steps, and outfield players used to come and hit you. The keepers today have it so soft; they can run where they want and pass the ball. True to form, the defender rushed in and flattened David. Of course, the referee gave us a penalty. David stepped up and put it away, so we won 3-2. He had brains!

In the final, we were playing midweek. On that particular night, half our players couldn't make it. David was one of them. We were beaten in the final. Many years later, a friend stopped me and said, "Pete, I saw a picture of you in David Lloyd's new book." Sure enough, there is a picture of the football team in his autobiography, which was published in 2001. That is my claim to fame! After that, they stopped David from playing football because of the danger of him getting injured, and the team basically fell apart.

The cricket team for which I had previously played at Langbridge while serving my apprenticeship had gone bust by this time. The set-up for cricket teams was more spread out than for football, so the only team I could find nearby was with the Blackburn YMCA, which I had played against a few times in the past. I joined them, and I remember getting some decent scores. I also joined their football team. Again, they had three teams, and I went straight into the second team. I was playing out at full back by this time, having decided that I'd had enough of being in goal, and was doing very well. The third team was made up of veterans, all over the age of 30. As I was nearing that milestone, I decided to ask if I could join them, and I did. It was great, just guys enjoying their football and enjoying playing together. The first team had a goalkeeper, a big lad who wasn't bad. One game he could not play, so they asked me to step in. Reluctantly, I agreed and played in goal for them. We made a draw, and I played well. They wanted me to carry on with them, but obviously I refused. I wanted to get back to the good lads in the veterans. We got used to passing the ball, similar to 'two-touch' football, and it was nice. One particular Saturday, the first team had no game on, and they came to us and asked if we would play two of their main players in our squad. We let them come in, and, well, they were rubbish! They just wanted to dribble. I was the captain, and I spent all the time shouting at them to pass! It was a joke; they were terrible. Constant dribbling was all they had been doing in the first team – no wonder they didn't win anything! Don't get me wrong, they were good players, but they had no football sense.

During the last full season, we ran away with the league and were doing well in the cup. We got to the cup final, and then we had a dilemma. Our goalkeeper had lost his nerve due to being badly hurt as he went out for a ball. He was really flattened. We didn't have a replacement, so we just had to play him when he got fit again. During the last quarter of the season, we were winning games by scores like 7-5 or 6-4. Luckily, we could score more goals than our opposition, so we were able to keep winning. On the selection night before the cup final, I just said, "Look, I'm sorry, but we just can't risk him. It's too important a game. I'll go in goal instead." Everyone agreed, and our usual keeper became the substitute. We only had 12 players in the squad and would rotate being the sub. We won the game 3-0. The cup was ours, and we did the double!

Terry, one of our players and a good friend of mine, worked at the same factory as the team we played. Of course, the next day, he went into work and was taking the mickey out of them. He later came back and told me that the thing that upset them about losing was that we had dropped our usual keeper. They were relying on just hammering shots at the keeper as their main strategy. When they saw that I was in goal, and some of them knew me from years before in the Accrington leagues, where I had been a good keeper, they were demoralised!

The next season started off OK, and the first team wanted to pinch a few of our players, as we had a couple of younger lads in who were good. They nicked them from us, which was something we could not stop. During one of the early games of that season, I got a really bad injury, and I did not play again for a long time. It was a really heavy tackle that swept the bottom half of my leg and injured my knee. The next day, I hobbled down to hospital on a broom as a crutch with my knee all swollen up. I saw an Asian lady doctor. She didn't even X-ray it or anything, just bandaged me up and that was it.

When I was back in Zambia, I would go to clubs and people would come in with guitars to perform. You would ask them to play some of your favourite songs, and they would say, "How does it go? You sing it and I'll play it." It made me realise that I would like to learn how to play the guitar. Back in England, I met up with a guy I knew called Pete Gardner. He was a lot bigger than me and was known as 'Big Pete'. He had been playing in local bands from the late 1950s onwards and was good. He lived in Barnoldswick, not far from where I was working in Earby. On my way home from work, I started to call round at his house, and he would show me a few chords on the guitar. I had bought a cheap second-hand guitar, and I would go home and practise. I never got good enough to join his band though. I got very friendly with Big Pete; in fact, he would later be my best man at my wedding to Shirley, and we are still in touch now.

In 1969, I met Shirley Woodworth, who was later to become my wife. She was 19 and I was 29. We met in a pub called The Bridge in Accrington. I was there for a drink with a friend of mine called John. John and I had been apprentices and played football together in the past. I kept looking across at her and then she came across and spoke to me. I was still very shy. She was there with a friend who fancied John, but he was shy like me. I don't remember buying her a drink, but we made a date to meet up again. Shirley worked in a bank in a nearby town and would work there for seven years in all before she decided to go to college in Manchester and become a teacher. Back in 1969, we dated for a short while, but we both realised that we were not ready to settle down. I was still restless, and we went our different ways.

Around this time, my dad decided he wanted to retire. As I have said before, he was a clever man. He had spotted the potential of spiral tubing way back. He talked to his partner in Bell Metals about it. Together they found out about a guy called Wells who was importing this tubing from Switzerland. My dad and Bell took Wells on as a partner. The three of them then went over to Switzerland and bought the machines that made the tubing. This guy Wells turned out to be a rogue. He said to my dad that they should get rid of Bell from the partnership, and my dad refused, as he was very straight and honest. Wells then got to Bell, and between them they bought out my dad. Then Wells did the dirty on Bell and basically kicked him out. Bell ended up with nothing from the company, and it killed him really; he just faded away and died. Wells started a big factory in Keighley called Wells Spiral Tubes.

After all that, my dad eventually decided that he wanted

to go back to Huddersfield and play golf, so he sold up his business. I didn't have the money to buy it, so I started up my own engineering workshop. I got the basic equipment I needed no problem, and I got plenty of work locally. I used to get work from all the towns in the area, and I was doing all right. I was doing small fabrication jobs, and if it involved machining, I could farm it out to another company that was in another part of the same building. One of the main companies I was dealing with was G-Plan furniture. They had a big factory in Nelson, and I was making the jigs for them. I also used to do all their repairs. I was in with a couple of big mills too, carrying out repairs and making guards and things like that.

Then came the three-day week as a result of the miners' strike, which started in December 1973. It did not affect me, because I could hire myself out to companies that needed me, but it was a really bad time for a lot of people. I could see the writing on the wall in terms of how long it was going to take for things to recover. Just then, I spotted advertisements for work in Zambia in the national papers, and I decided to go back.

This is the football team that David Lloyd's dad ran. I'm fourth from the left in the back row and David is fourth from the left in the front row.

CHAPTER SIX
Back to Zambia

They took me back on at the same mine in Luanshya in late 1974. This time, I had a house and was not in bachelor quarters. I also took my guitar with me. I was working in the concentrator area, where we crushed the ore, and I got friendly with the engineer there. He was a typical university lout. He played the guitar too and sang as loud as anybody. He was called Dave and was from somewhere in Yorkshire. He was a great guy, one of those who would get up on a table and start playing and singing without hesitation. There was another guy called Bill who also played and sang and who worked with us too. Bill had been a club singer, so he knew all the popular songs and the chords. We used to jam together. The hardest place to play was the rugby club, where there were some really tough guys. They knew every song going. While we would be playing away, they would sometimes come up and throw buckets of water over us. Our strings used to break like crazy. One night, I ended up with just two strings left!

I then managed to get the job of assistant foreman in the main fabrication shop. The foreman was Scottish. For some reason, he just did not like me. I can get on with anybody, but he just did not take to me. At one time, we were having a big event on the lake and wanted to have a raft race. We had about three or four weeks to prepare. I said to the foreman, "Right, let's get going, let's make a raft." He was having none of it; he said we could not take part. It was a massive mine, and people from all the different departments were going to take part. I asked him umpteen times if we could enter, and he always said no. I heard from my engineer friend, Dave, who was still in the concentrator department, that he was really disappointed that we were not making a raft. Bugger that! I had three young lads working under me, and I told them that on Saturday morning we were coming in and were going to make a raft. They were all for it. We finished making it on Sunday morning, and then we painted it with a shark's face on the front. We got it up on a wagon with about an hour to spare. When we got to the lake, there was every type of raft you could think of. Some guys had put together four bathtubs (they were all four-man rafts), with a guy sat in each tub rowing. One of the funniest ones was made of 45gal. drums with a platform on top. On the platform they had put a table and four chairs complete with a tablecloth! When the race started, they pulled the tablecloth off, pulled out the beers and sat around the table drinking.

We did not win the race. The guy who did was a proper professional oarsman. He and his team had built a proper rowing boat and had been out on the lake for weeks practising. Our raft was still there on the lake for ages after the race. People just used to use it to play on. The foreman never said anything about the fact I had gone against his instruction. He was a pillock. At one point, he went off on holiday for a month, and, in his absence, I got that place running so great. He had no idea what he was doing; he just sat in his office all the time. He was not a hands-on person.

At this particular time, Southern Rhodesia was doing really well. They had to knuckle down and make everything themselves, as there was still nothing coming through from outside due to the embargo on Rhodesia, which was a main trade route.

One of the towns, Kitwe, had a lot of wine delivered at around Christmastime. A crowd of us set off to go there and buy some of the wine. You were only allowed two bottles: one red and one white. God, that wine was strong. The red was like sherry. A crowd of us sat round a table drinking a bottle of the white, and we were soon all drunk! It had been imported from China.

One of the guys who worked on the mine had a cafe in town with his wife. Sometimes I would go down there and have a nice meal. On Saturday mornings, we all used to order pies from him. These were special curry pies. On Friday nights, the cafe would have a curry night, and any of the leftovers would go into the pies. They were beautiful. The Africans called it a 'pie meat' rather than a 'meat pie'.

One day, I had an encounter with African killer bees. I came home from work, and, for some reason I could not understand, there were quite a lot of bees in the house. Of course, you always kept a decent insect spray to hand, so I sprayed and killed them. There are that many nasties that will hurt you out there that you need something powerful to combat them. Everything seemed fine until night-time, when I was taking the rubbish out to the bin. The bins hung in a tree, mainly because there were always packs of dogs about. If the bin were to be left on the ground, the dogs would tip it over and ransack it. The dogs often used to belong to people who had worked there and who had now gone home and left their dog behind. I never had one; I did not want one. As I was walking out to the bin this night, I heard a humming noise. I just lifted my bin lid up, and all these bees suddenly rose up. I dropped the bin lid and ran like hell back to the house.

About an hour or two later, I decided I had to put that lid back on. Armed with my insect spray, I sneaked out, picked up the lid, stuck it on the bin and ran like the clappers back to the house. The next morning, having forgotten all about it, I opened the back door to head out to the car. I saw a slight movement, and, when I looked closer, the only way I can describe what I saw is like an ice cream cone with the ice cream flowing down the sides. The bees were hanging halfway down the bin, millions of them. As soon as I got into work at 6am, I phoned up the townships (the people who sorted stuff like that out) and told them what was going on. When I finished work at 3pm, I rushed home as quickly as I could. The tree was dead. They had killed the tree. There were millions of bees on the floor, and it took me ages to shovel them up and put them in the bin. I asked the neighbours if they had seen anything. They said yes and told me that when the bees had escaped, they had flown into the next garden. The exterminators had followed them down the street, spraying the trees. Everybody had dead trees, but it had cured the problem!

Whilst working on the mine, there were always contractors working there doing jobs too. The contracting companies would always ask us if we would like to earn extra money by taking a week or so of leave from the mine and taking on a job through them for cash in hand. They always needed a white face to run the operations. Finally,

I agreed and put in for two weeks' leave. The company boss drove me out to Lusaka, the capital of Zambia. He showed me the job, which was at a cement works on the outskirts of the city. It was taking down some massive 20ft-diameter tanks on concrete plinths. There were four of them, and behind them was a big wall and all the pipelines for the cement works. Then there was a conveyor system to take down, but you could not get at it for these four tanks, so they had to come down first.

I arrived on a Saturday morning, and they put me up in a motel not far away. They promised me that, within a few days, a wagon would arrive with a gang of African labourers, ladders, cutting gear and a crane. Sunday came and nothing happened. On Monday, a pick-up arrived with one of the drivers, which was fine. On Tuesday, nothing happened. I drove to the cement works and telexed the company. They were full of apologies. Wednesday came, and finally a truck arrived with a gang of labourers but no gear. I contacted the company through the telex again, and they just said to me, "Go out and hire, buy or steal what you need." Luckily, they gave me some working capital. Off on the wagon with some of the crew, we trawled Lusaka looking for whatever we could buy, hire, find or steal. We managed to get enough equipment to make a start. On Thursday, we finally began. I then got a message to go and find a low-loader wagon to meet up with the crane at the station of a town about 100mi. away. The train was bringing a cherry-picker for us. I set off again to find transport for the cherry-picker. I found a low-loader and sent the crane driver with it to go and collect the crane.

We carried on splitting the tanks into 10ft sections. On each section, we would put holes along the edge so that we could put shackles in and pick them up with the crane. On Friday, I was called out again to get some more gear, and when I arrived back in the afternoon, I could see all the boys lined up at the gates as I drove back towards the cement works. Oh God, this was trouble. What had they done? I asked what had happened. They had decided to cut out a piece of one of the tanks. Instead of cutting it out at the front and letting it fall, they had cut it out at the back. It had landed against the pipes, which were a foot or two in diameter, and knocked all three of them down; the main slurry line, the main water line and another line carrying something else. The cement works was shut down! We had to start then and find pipe to repair them and weld them into place. We got it done, and I headed back to my digs at about 10pm. I had been so busy that I had not eaten all day and was starving.

The manager of the motel said, "I'm sorry, we're shut. You can't have any food."

I replied, "You had better give me some food. I'm dying here!"

They refused, and I told them I would blacken their name with every company I could so that nobody would stay there. As we were arguing back and forth, I could see that there was a mirror just to the side of the door. I noticed that the crane driver was standing there. Oh great, the crane had arrived. I asked the crane driver if it was outside.

"No, boss, it didn't fit the low-loader."

I asked him what he meant by saying that it didn't fit. It had fallen off! I asked him if the crane was upright or horizontal, and he confirmed that it was on its side. I told him that I was going to pick him up at 4am, and we would drive down to see what we could do.

The motel fed me, and I arranged for them to wake me up early. I picked up the driver, and we made the 100mi. journey to the railway sidings, where, sure enough, the crane was on its side. There was oil, diesel, hydraulic fluid and you name it all over the place. We drove around to see if we could find anybody who could hire us a crane to pick it up. Nothing. Nobody had a crane; nobody would lend us a crane or anything. There was a small copper mine about 30 or 40mi. away. We drove out there, and, believe you me, it took a bit of begging and eating humble pie to persuade the engineers to lend me a crane. They finally agreed and said that it would be there at about 3pm. It arrived at the railway sidings and picked up the fallen crane no problem. In the meantime, I had telexed again to ask for a mechanic and diesel oil to be sent to fix this bloody crane. I gave the guys from the copper mine what money I had left as payment for righting the crane. I had been cleaned out by then from buying and hiring all this equipment.

After that, I just drove back to Luanshya, which was a long drive, and wrote out a full report saying that I'd had enough and was quitting. I put it through the letterbox of the boss of this contracting firm at about 6am and then went to bed. I was woken up in the afternoon by the boss begging me to go back and finish the job. He gave me some more working capital and a promise that the crane would be sorted and back on the road to Lusaka. I left early Monday morning to head back to the railway siding to see what was happening there. The maintenance crew had arrived and had started to sort out the crane, and they soon got it running again. When I saw that they had it running, I set off back in the direction of Lusaka.

After about 60mi., I stopped and thought I had better go

back and check. Sure enough, it was stuck at the side of the road, with hydraulic oil pouring out all over the place. The mechanics had left, so I had to drive to the copper mine again and telex the company again, saying that the next mechanic who came out had to stay with the crane until the journey's end. Then I drove back to the cement works and told the men to down tools and have a rest. Then I went back and stayed with the crane until it was fixed and back on its way. However, as it was being driven along the road, it was chugging along, only doing about 15–20mph. I stayed with it all the way until it arrived late Friday afternoon. Well, we tore down every piece of those tanks in record time.

Late Saturday night, I set off home and wrote another report, which I put through the letterbox of the boss, then I went back to my usual job on Monday morning! As a footnote to this, the contracting company gave me an added bonus for all the hardships on top of what they were paying me. Much later on, I saw the company boss and asked how they had got on with the job to take down the conveyor system. He said that they had managed to get it down, but they had toppled the crane over again while doing it! At that, I just walked away before he could see me laughing!

A proper holiday I took while in Zambia was a flight up to stay on Lake Tanganyika. It is the longest lake in the world, around 410mi., and the second deepest. Four countries touch its shores: Zaire (now the Democratic Republic of the Congo), Burundi, Tanzania and Zambia. Besides fish, it is also home to crocodiles, hippos, fish eagles and lots of wildlife. The main reason people used to go up there was to fish for tiger fish. I don't know much about fishing. The only fishing I had ever done was for sticklebacks when I was a kid!

After leaving the plane, I was taken by Land Rover to where I was staying at Nkamba Lodge. The journey was horrendously bumpy. My camera was in a bag, which fell on the floor, and it was bouncing around. Where we were on this little camp, there was a beautiful stretch of the lakeside, where all the animals used to come, but my camera had been knocked out of focus by the bumpy journey! I was so annoyed, because I couldn't take any pictures of them. I saw a sign which said you could put your name down for a walking safari leaving at 4am. I asked if I could put my name down, and the guy said, "I'm sorry, boss, but we've only got one bullet left. If we miss, we're dead!" Until the next shipment of bullets arrived, they could not run any more walking safaris.

We were staying in nice little round thatched buildings, but at night the hippos used to come and rub themselves on the sides of the hut. The hut would be shaking, and the hippos would be grunting. There was no way you wanted to go outside while they were there. The next day, the water pump broke, and there was no water. They said that they would take us to the next camp in Kasaba Bay. That was a lovely camp with nice big square houses and a nice big restaurant. The first night there, I was heading down to the restaurant for a meal. Suddenly, a herd of elephants came through and ripped most of the gauze off of the restaurant windows trying to get at the food. This one woman's husband was still in his cabin getting ready when he heard the elephants coming through. He stepped out onto the veranda with his camera, and an elephant's trunk knocked it out of his hand! Our next incident was with monkeys, which just came down and grabbed everything they could.

Kasaba Bay was nice, with lots of fishing boats. I noticed

a tiny little sign saying 'Beware of crocodiles', and when I looked – bloody hell – there was one right there! How dangerous was that? There was no fence or anything! They used to take us out in the Land Rover to different stretches of the lakeside, where there were beaches and no crocodiles. You could swim there, and in the distance you could see elephants coming down. Then we would get back in the Land Rover and head back. One particular day, they dropped us off, and the guy said, "We are going to have to leave you here, because we need to use the Land Rover to collect some supplies, but we will leave an armed guard with you." I don't know how many bullets he had. The group of five or six of us went off and had a swim, then we got dressed and ready to leave. We were heading up a path, and, when we looked at the ground, we saw all these footprints. They were animal pawprints. We asked the guard what animal had made them, and he said, "Looks like a hyena." We saw more and asked about those, to which he said, "That could be a leopard." All the time, we were crowding closer and closer to the armed guard. He had become our best buddy! With every noise we could hear in the bush, we thought it could be one of those dangerous animals. We made it back safely that day.

    On another morning, another holidaymaker and I went out fishing. We went out early at about 5am. This guy had a wife and a couple of kids with him, and they were going swimming. When we got back, they told us that while they were swimming, a hippo had come up out of the water behind them and they had run off screaming. If that hippo had had a youngster with it, it would have attacked and killed them. When they got to the guard, they found him fast asleep under a tree.

As I said, I am not a fisherman, and while we were out in the boat, the guy said to me, "What we are doing today is bottom fishing." We just had sticks with string and about five or six hooks on each. We had two Africans with us to paddle the boat. We would watch for where the birds were coming down in the water to get small fish. That was a sign that there would be bigger fish below, and that was where we would head to drop our lines. We were pulling out two or three fish at a time, and within an hour we had filled the bottom of the boat with fish. It was unbelievable! That fish was beautiful barbecued.

In Zambia, as with many other African countries, I would often be visited by lads offering to do menial jobs for me. I always refused as best I could. I would listen to them talk and then send them away. At one point, I had a big delivery of gravel for my driveway dropped off. It was a massive pile. I left it sitting there; I could not be bothered to deal with it right away. Then, shortly after, this young lad came and asked me for a job. I said I didn't want anybody, but he replied, "Let me put your gravel down." I told him it was too big a job, but he insisted that he would show me how good he was by doing it. He laid it in a single day, so I gave him a chance and hired him full-time.

All the houses had a lot of land attached. At the bottom of each garden was a kia, which was the house for your African servant. He moved into the kia at the bottom of my garden. I used to give him seeds, and he would grow all sorts for me. He was a really good lad, nice and well-spoken. He was in his early 20s and lived in the kia with his wife and baby. He did so well that I bought him a new Chinese bicycle at Christmas.

Then, one day, when he had been working for me for

quite a while, he was arrested on a trumped-up charge of robbery. It seemed to have come about over somebody wanting his wife. This other person, the one who wanted his wife, was a relation of the chief of police. I got him a lawyer, and we fought the case. I was a witness to where he was at the particular time in question. I told the court that on that Saturday night, I had seen him, and he had been dressed in his best clothes, which were white. Would you go robbing dressed in white? Everything was to no avail, and they sentenced him to something like 12 months and put him in a chain gang. We tried everything we could to help him, and I visited him a couple of times while he was out working in the fields as part of the chain gang. His wife and child stayed living in the kia in my garden, and she took over some of his chores, such as tending to the garden. When I left Zambia, he still had not been released.

I have tried to be honest all my life and to take people at face value until they prove otherwise. This was a good lad who worked hard all day. The police were terrible in Zambia at that time, and everyone was corrupt. When I was working down in the main workshops, one of the boys down there was taken away by the police, and the Africans with whom I worked told me about him. I don't know the crime with which he was charged, but by the time they finally released him, they had shaved the soles off his feet to make him talk. That is how bad it was. The guy could not walk.

Another example of corruption was the driving test we had to take when working at the mine. You had to have a Zambian licence, and we would go down to the driving test centre in a Morris Minor pick-up truck. There were always a few ex-pats there on certain days, perhaps five or six of us. The centre had quite a big area where they would set out

50gal. drums, between which we had to reverse from either side. We were all there early and could see that the drums were scattered everywhere. They had been knocked into and left. A group of us set them all straight and lined them up. When the examiner came, he made us move them back to where they had been! They had left rings in the earth, so we could see where to return them to. What a nags up.

After you had passed that section of it, then the fun started. They placed a chair on the back of the pick-up for the examiner to sit on and shout instructions to us. The police inspector would sit next to the driver. He was there to stop bribery, which was rife. Mind you, it wasn't by us ex-pats; it was mainly the Africans. We ex-pats had all been driving for years already. While the person being tested was out driving around the streets, the examiner would be leaning around, shouting out where to go: "Turn left here!" "Turn right!" "Stop!" etc. Needless to say, I got my Zambian licence with no problems, but it was like something from the Keystone Cops.

One time, a load of people from the Congress Party came into Luanshya for some kind of promotion. They were there for a week and took over a girls' school. They made those girls be their slaves for the duration of their stay. It was terrible; I hate to think what happened to those poor girls.

All locals were paid at the end of the month, and it could be hard for them to make their wages last through until the next payday. That meant that, in the last week of the month, you had to be on the lookout for the stunts they would pull to try to get money off you. Such efforts also applied to the corrupt police, as I found out one day when I was arrested. At the end of each working day, there would be a race to get out of the gates first. This particular day, the colleague with whom I shared a car and I were out of the gate second. We got to a T-junction on our way out of the main mine area. Going straight ahead would take us to town, while turning left would take us to the residential area. To the right was just a little cemetery where some of the early settlers were buried. I visited the cemetery once, and it was sad to see how young many of the people had been when they had died, including a lot of babies. The traffic leaving the mine that day was all turning left, heading for home. We went about a quarter of a mile down the road when the police jumped out of the trees in front of us, holding guns. They stopped all the cars. The lucky ones at the back could see what was happening and were able to turn around and sneak off in the other direction. When we asked them why they had stopped us, they said it was because we had not stopped at the T-junction. You could hardly see the T-junction from this point; it was a quarter of a mile away! It was not even a stop sign, just a give way sign. Nevertheless, they arrested us all, the occupants of about 12 or 15 cars. They positioned a police car at the front, one at the back, and then drove us out of town to the African township police station, which was a long way away. As we were driving along, if we passed a street leading off to the side, a car from the middle would shoot off. By the time we got to the police station, there were only about six cars left in the line. On the way there, they also arrested a bus at a junction we passed. The bus had stopped at the junction, as it was supposed to, but, while stationary, people were jumping on and off the bus, which was not allowed. The police arrested the driver, and we ended up in procession behind this bus, which was jam packed full of passengers!

When we finally arrived at the police station, the people

on the bus were going mad, because they were now nowhere near where they wanted to be going. It was an African police station in the mid 1970s, so it was not very nice. They took us all upstairs and proceeded to fine the drivers. I was not driving that day, but of course we all chipped in and pooled whatever money we had to cover the fines, which I think was something like 15 kwacha each (about £8). The police gave one person permission to go out and get some more money, while the rest of us had to wait there until he came back. What a way for the police to make money, eh?

Another time, I had to take a newcomer to the police station to register a car he had bought. I took him to the police station in the town, which was quite a nice big station. We pulled up, and as we walked towards the doors, they burst open, and every cop in the building ran out. There must have been 15 or 20 of them, and they were carrying every conceivable weapon you can imagine: rifles, pistols, shotguns etc. They jumped into various cars, vans and trucks and flew off. We were stood there gobsmacked. There were guns sticking out of every police vehicle window. Some officers were in uniform and others in plain clothes. When they had gone, we walked into the station to find it completely empty, not a soul in sight. We shouted but received no answer. We made our way upstairs, still shouting, and eventually we found a clerk right at the back. We had to basically force him to sign the document this newcomer needed, as it was the last day he had to register the car. We asked the clerk what was happening and where the officers had gone. He told us there had been a robbery in town, and they had gone to investigate! As we were driving back through the town, we saw them riding around in a convoy.

Again, it was just like the Keystone Cops!

As we reached 1975, we were invaded by the army, who set up roadblocks on the way in and out of every town. The copper belt has a straight road running from Lusaka up to the Congo. All the towns in the copper belt lead off this main road. Luanshya was near the bottom, and if we ever needed anything from another town, we got there via this main road. It became an ordeal, because to get anywhere we had to pass through the roadblock on the way out of Luanshya, then through the roadblock on the way into the town to which we were going, then it was the same in reverse on our way back. It could take hours, with cars lined up waiting to pass through. The cars would all be thoroughly checked, but if you asked what they were looking for, they would never tell you. One of my friends was checked at a roadblock, and they found that his wipers were not working. He got away with it by saying, "Don't be daft; they only work when it's raining!" Another poor guy, who had just come in from England, tried to pass through a roadblock while wearing a beautiful big watch on his wrist. Well, they took one look at that watch and arrested him for being a spy! They swore blind that it was a radio watch that he could talk into and send messages. Nobody saw that bloke for about a month afterwards. When he came out, although he had not been tortured, he was not the same lad that he had been.

One day, I was in the queue at a roadblock, waiting to go through. It took a long time for them to search through the boot and any luggage etc., so you could be queuing for quite a while. As the queue moved forwards, I pulled up alongside this guy wearing sergeant stripes. He was holding a revolver and a rusty F-spanner. I do not know what he was doing, but he was messing about somehow and a bullet dropped out. He looked at me, then bent down, picked it up and put it back in the gun. This happened another few times. I was starting to get worried, because he was looking meaner and meaner and starting to get annoyed at dropping the bullets because he was embarrassed and angry. Finally, before he shot me, the queue moved forwards and I got away intact. Boy, was I thankful!

Another time, while I was waiting at the roadblock, the army opened the boot of a car a few cars in front of me in the queue and found a rifle. Well, they dragged the guy out of the car and had him up against a tree. Of course, the guy did not know anything about it, but he was lucky they didn't shoot him there and then. After a while, they realised that the rifle must have been planted there at the last roadblock. Finally, they sent a Land Rover to where he had been, which took another hour or more with us all still in the queue behind him. The Land Rover came back with a sheepish looking private who had put his gun down in the boot while searching the car at the last roadblock and accidentally left it there. They didn't half give him hell.

There were a lot of robberies all over the place, and a lot of people had dogs for security. One robbery which occurred was at one of the clubs one Saturday night. A gang of masked Africans burst in and demanded money from the till. The bar people were always ready, having put all the change into crisp tins. In the old days, you used to get a tin of crisps about 12in. square. When the robbers came in, they would find the tins, shake them, hear the rattle and be happy to make off with the contents. This particular night, the gang burst in, and the leader was shouting, wanting money. Somebody moved over near the door, and the leader turned and fired, killing one of his own men. The rest of the gang just quickly dragged him out and left. Most of these thieves had come down from the Congo, where people were a lot poorer than in Zambia.

A couple of my friends were burgled one evening. The robbers broke in, brandishing guns and machetes, which was terrifying. My friends tried to be friendly to them and gave them whatever money they had and whatever possession they wanted. They even made them food. Finally, the robbers left without harming them. They were so lucky. I don't think they stayed in the country much longer after that. Zambia just was not the same place as it had been before. Independence had given rise to so much corruption and so many problems. It was such a beautiful country, like paradise, at least to us ex-pats.

One of the only remaining good things by this time was when we got to play and sing together, going to perform at parties at night. One do we organised was a Liverpool night. A lot of people made scouse, a traditional Liverpool dish, which is basically a stew with every vegetable you can think of. One of the engineers was a brilliant pianist. He used to play The Entertainer by Scott Joplin, which featured in the film The Sting. He did not have the music; he could just play it by ear, and it was amazing. We roped him into our Liverpool night. I made the music stands, and I got the words and chords for every Liverpool song we could think of. Then I prepared a second set, which was all just Beatles songs.

We played the first set, the Liverpool set, with everybody joining in singing. It was brilliant. Then we had the scouse and a few drinks. What I had forgotten was that the engineer got drunk easily. After four beers, he was totally drunk. The beer was strong; I had to limit myself to four beers in fact because after that I could not remember what I was doing. Friends of mine had been found crawling out of town on their hands and knees they were that badly drunk. After the break, we got up to start the second set. All the songs were in order on the music stand. The engineer took one look and decided he did not like that one. He started going through the song sheets, casting the ones he didn't like onto the floor until he found one he was happy to start playing. Oh my God, it was chaos. We were all trying to wing it from there, trying to work out what key he was playing in. We got through most of it, and, in the end, it was a great show. People enjoyed it, because of course they could see what was going on.

It was getting harder and harder to live in Zambia, with the police and the army really making it tough and there being bandits about. Even leaving the mine had become hard work by 1975. They had put security on every exit from the mine, so we now had another queue to wait in to be searched before leaving the site.

One day, I was going through one of the bush roads, and I came across this dead legavaan, which is a type of rock monitor lizard. It was about four feet long and looked like a crocodile, with a long face, but it had a big, forked tongue. I put it in the boot of my car, and when I got home, I spent some time propping it in the boot in just the right way so that when the boot was opened, the head and front legs would pop out. The next time I was in the queue at the checkpoint and they asked me to open the boot, I said, "Are you sure?"

The guard said, "Yes, open it now."

I did, and the legavaan jumped out just as I had intended. The three of them ran off screaming! We all got a free pass through the checkpoint that day, with them shouting, "Move, go through, move now!" The next afternoon, there was a different set of guards on duty. Again, when I was asked to open the boot, I said, "Are you sure?" Same thing all over again: they ran off screaming. They never stopped me again after that. After about four days, the lizard started to smell terrible, so I ended up chucking it out in the bush.

Back in the 1960s, everybody used to help each other, and if anyone needed anything, there was a community there to pitch in. For example, I had been involved in making garden swing sets for people, fabricating the uprights while someone else made the seat bars, and someone else made the seat slats etc. It was a collaborative effort of a group of people working to do something helpful. Nobody wanted money; it was just a sideline for anyone who wanted a swing in their garden. We also made barbecues. People just mucked in, and it was great. That had all stopped.

Around this time, I started to realise that it was no fun to live and work there any more; it was just hassle. It was time to leave. The bosses understood why I wanted to leave; in fact, many of them were leaving themselves. The whole situation was terrible.

When I went back to the UK to live with my mum, I went into a newsagents' shop and got the biggest shock of my life. All the shelves were full with cigarettes, crisps, sweets, newspapers and magazines. It just blew me away, and I stood there just staring. It was such a contrast to Zambia, where the shops were practically empty, with nothing on the shelves.

I did not stay long, just two or three weeks. I then received a letter from Dave, the engineer whom I had met in Zambia at the start of 1974. He said that he had got a job in Sierra Leone and asked if I would like to go out there. I didn't know anything about it, but I headed off to Leeds for an interview and a medical, then I packed my bags and my guitar and flew out. In the meantime, while I was at home, I met up with Shirley again on a night out at a club somewhere. We acknowledged that we still liked each other, but I then left the country again. She had become a teacher by then, and we each had our own lives.

The bin with the bees

Me, Bill and Dave, the engineer, playing at a Christmas party

One of the fish I caught on lake Tanganyika

CHAPTER SEVEN
Sierra Leone

The name Sierra Leone comes from the Portuguese explorers who, passing the hills, thought it had the look of a sleeping lion. When you look at the bulge on the west coast of Africa, Sierra Leone is about three quarters of the way down it. It was well known for the slave trade, as in the centre of Freetown, the capital, was a very large tree where slaves used to be chained up while waiting to be shipped out. The name Freetown came about when slavery was starting to be abolished in around 1787. England sent ships full of slaves, and I believe also transported a ship full of prostitutes and felons out there as well. They started to colonise the place, and that was how it became a 'free town'. A lot of slaves came from Nova Scotia as well, and they all stayed in Freetown. They ended up being a very clever race of Africans, educated better than most. Lots of them became doctors, lawyers, engineers etc., many with double-barrelled names. They were called the Krio. In America, there are Creoles in Louisiana and the South; this is the same name but spelt differently. They made up their own language, which was a mixture of English and other languages but was understandable and became a universal language throughout. All Africans could speak it as well as their own tribal language. There were also bush Africans, from the Mende and Temne tribes. They were less well educated.

Like everywhere in Africa, tribalism is everything. That was why you used to have so many coups going on across the continent.

You would have one tribe saying, "We're not having them running us," and they would do their best to get rid of them.

The company for which I went to work as a supervisor was called Sierra Rutile. It was owned by an American company called Bethlehem Steel, which was the biggest steel-making company in America at the time. From the mineral rutile you get titanium dioxide and titanium monoxide. One of them makes titanium, and the other makes pigments for paints and the coating for welding rods. There were other minerals too, but they were mainly after the titanium. The area had previously been dredged back in the 1950s by another American-owned company. They had used a screw dredge, which had buried in, but I don't think they had got the amount out that they had wanted. It wasn't viable to do it using the screw method, so they had abandoned it.

Bethlehem Steel was building a floating dredge in cooperation with Taylor Woodrow and had already built a floating washing plant and another dry processing plant. They were about a quarter of the way through building the dredge when I got there.

It was a massive plant employing hundreds of Africans, including several Krio engineers, and there was a man-made lake where the ore was in the banks. We had a big power shop with generators for the electricity needed to run everything and a huge workshop for all the D8s, D6s and D4s – the heavy vehicles. They are like big diggers with tank-like tracks. They also had a big machine shop and a motor vehicle shop.

My role was supervisor of the big workshop for fabrication and welding. In the workshop, I had three foremen at that time, all local bush Africans. Their names were Joe Moody (the general foreman), Patrick Sheriff and Young Joe (because this Joe was younger than Moody, we gave him the nickname Young Joe). Then there was a team of about 30 Africans working under them. I had to split them into two groups, one half going to the dredge and the other half in the workshop. They were hard work to manage, as were the Krio engineers. They often did not want to listen to the experience that the other white employees and I had to share. I had been in Zambia and working in the mining industry for years, but they had come out of university and felt that they knew what they were doing without advice from anyone else.

The camp was built in the style of American summerhouses: single storey, with plenty of gauze over the windows and doors to keep the flies out but let the air through. The furniture was top quality. All the kitchen equipment – copper-bottomed pots and pans etc. – were all the best too. We bachelors lived in a row of self-contained accommodation where we each had our own cooker, bedroom, shower room and office area. I used to get my meals at the mess restaurant. A bus was provided every day, a very old bus, just like an American school bus but older. It would take us to work each morning, bring us back for lunch, take us back to work for the afternoon and then bring us home again at the end of the day. It was a four- or five-kilometre journey on a dirt road up and down a hill. The camp area was beautiful, with a bar, restaurant, shop, library, sports area with pool tables and a bowling alley and an indoor area where films were shown (once a month if we were lucky). There was also a large outdoor area.

Life on the camp was great. Most nights we would go down to the bar with the Taylor Woodrow guys and would drink and sing songs. At weekends, it would be more or less a similar story, plus swimming in the Olympic-sized pool. There were always kids about who had come to visit their parents during school holidays, and the married guys all had their wives living on the camp with them.

There was a bauxite mine about 30mi. away from us. We used to alternate Sunday visits: one week they would come to us for a swim and a party, then the next weekend we would go over there and do the same. Their camp was not quite as nice as ours – it was a bit more primitive with fewer amenities – but it was all right. Bauxite ore makes aluminium, and the bauxite mine was owned by a Swiss company called Alusuisse and run under the company name Sieromco. The first weekend of every month, we used to have a curry Sunday, and white European people used to come from miles around for it. It was a really good social time. The camp restaurant and its black staff would do the cooking.

Once a month, the mail would arrive. With it would come newspapers: The Times, The Observer etc. We were not interested in the newspapers, but the people who ran the mine would be. One particular Thursday night, I was there when the mail arrived. We had a brilliant idea to make the best paper hats we could out of the newspapers. Well, we went to town with them! It was a proper competition to make the best hat. We wrecked the newspapers, obviously, but it was a great night, and we had some fun. When we had finished, one of the guys rolled up a big sheet of newspaper, stuck it up his backside, lit it and ran off!

Every month or so we would get R&R (rest and recovery), and we would all go down to Freetown for a long weekend. We would fly down on a Friday, stay in our main offices down there and be back at the camp for work again on Monday. Up above our office there was a dormitory with eight or so rooms containing beds. Taylor Woodrow had the same, as did Sieromco. Any time we were going down, we would know who else was going to be in Freetown, so we would meet up and have a great time. There were only one or two high-rise buildings in Freetown then, but there was a big market where you could buy almost anything. When your batteries were charged up after the weekend, it was back to the grind at work.

It had been agreed that Taylor Woodrow would be there for the first six months that I was there, until they had finished off building the dredger, at which point they would leave. Every couple of months, their personnel would change, as they swapped out people who wanted to go home and brought in new people. Flights came in on a Saturday, no matter where you came from. They would have arrived in Freetown on the Friday and then got an inland flight to arrive at the camp the following day. The inland flights used Trislander planes, which had three propellers, one on the tail and one on each wing. They were powerful and could take off on a sixpence, basically. Sierra Leone is very delta, with lots of rivers and streams, and the weather alternated between six months dry and six months wet. As a consequence, the landing strips were only very small. We shared a landing strip nearby with Sieromco.

One particular Saturday, I recognised one of the young men arriving. I used to babysit for him and his wife when

I was an apprentice back in Accrington. He had come from Scotland originally and had then followed the work down to Accrington. He had been in the Black Watch and played the trumpet in the band. He was a nice guy. I can't remember his name unfortunately. I have never been very good with names, and it has got harder and harder as the years have gone on!

Down on the dredge, I would split the team into small groups of three or four and break each job into smaller tasks for them to do. I would try to get back round to check on them within an hour or an hour and a half, otherwise they would go past what I had explained and make a right mess. They were all right when working on smaller tasks, but when they got to thinking for themselves, it went wrong. It was just the same in the workshop. I would produce drawings for them to work from, and they would fabricate small jobs for me out of metal. Joe Moody, the general foreman, did not have a great brain, but he could manage the men well. He ruled the team with an iron fist, and it worked. Young Joe was keen and wanted to learn – a really nice lad. I would walk into the workshop and go by what I called 'rack of the eye'. I could cast my eye over all the jobs in there and tell straight away if something was not right or if it looked good. Joe Moody used to hate me coming in, because I would point out what was wrong with things. Later on, we got another supervisor who could keep an eye on things when I was on the dredge all the time, and that helped.

The dredge on which we were working was a bucket dredge, so the buckets would go down and dig, then come back up like a waterwheel. There were somewhere between 60 and 80 buckets on the dredge. The dredge had cables going out to either bank, and these were used to draw the dredge along. Think of it as like a lathe: the lathe chuck turns around fast and then you go along with the cutting tool. The dredge was in reverse of that. It was a massive piece of equipment. There were all types of equipment on that dredge. There was a massive ball mill. When the ore came from the buckets onto the conveyor system, it went straight into this ball mill, which would crush it up. We'd had the same ball mills on the copper belt, rows and rows of them. After the ball mill, the ore would then go through a series of other machines until, when it was like a slurry, it ran into a half-mile-long floating pipeline that led down to the washing plant, which was pulled behind the dredge. Once the ore was processed in the washing plant, it was piped again, this time to the shore and there was another big processing plant to get it down to the ore. The ore is very heavy and fine, and there is a lot of work involved in getting it out and processed to that stage.

One of the first jobs I had to do in Sierra Leone was make up the pipelines. The first part of the job was the two-foot-diameter pipe on top. The Africans had never done anything like that, so I had to make up a pipe square to help them make sure they did it right when putting the flanges on at the end. The next job was the tanks themselves, which were being made in Freetown. They came to us in the wrong shape, because they didn't have a clue how to roll them. I ended up having to go down and spend a few weeks training them. It is a tedious job: you feed the plate through gently, but the plate is eight feet long, and you have to go along the full length, tapping each bit. They got the hang of it in the end, but it was hard work. They would then send the tanks up to us at the mine when they had been tacked, and we would weld them and put the ends on. Then we had to put a saddle on so that the pipe would sit on top.

The first time they fired up the pipeline, ready to run ore through it, the torque was so high that it twisted the pipeline and sank the whole thing. The pipeline was made up of buoyancy tanks, 6ft in diameter and 20ft apart, with rubber pipes in-between, which allowed twist and flow. We had a large floating crane, which we used to try to recover the pipeline, but when we hooked it, the weight started pulling the crane under water. They stopped then and had a rethink. This guy, a fitter engineer called Pete Target, and I came up with an idea. We welded two of the six-foot-diameter tanks together and put valves on the top and lugs on either side so that we could tie ropes to them. We took them out to roughly the middle of where the pipeline had gone under and filled both tanks with water so that they sank down. Nobody else would go in, so I had to be the one to get into the lake and swim under the pipeline to get the two tanks central under the pipeline. Then I came up for air, went back down again and connected hoses to the valves to blow the water out and pump air into the tanks. Believe it or not, it succeeded in lifting the pipeline up. What a result! No medals were awarded though.

Dave, who had told me about Sierra Leone in the first place and who had been my boss originally, had been having marital problems and had left. The senior bosses had not had a clue what to do when the line sank, and at this particular point we did not have a senior engineer at all. When Dave's replacement did arrive, he was one of those who just sat at his desk. None of them had much of an idea from a practical point of view. I think the bosses respected me for what I was able to do, but they never showed it; they treated it as just another day's job to get on with. I did have total respect from the Africans though. They loved us. We treated them right and did not mess them around. Even when I had to knock down jobs they had done, we would build them back up again together, and they would learn from me. They even pinched a book I had on the development of metal work. I guess there might have been a cheer when the pipeline came up, but, as I was still under the water, I couldn't hear it if there was.

What everyone was scared of was what was in the water. There was one thing called a Guinea worm, which we called bilharzia, which could squirm up into your body (from a cut or anything), lay eggs inside you and then eat its way out. That could be very serious and really not very nice. That was just one of the reasons that nobody else would volunteer to get into the lake, which just left Joe Muggins here to do the dastardly deed. It wasn't that I was not scared of the parasites, it's just that there was nobody else!

After the pipeline had sunk, they were having a lot of other technical problems, and believe you me it was a headache. Everything used to go wrong, so the bosses, under advice, came to the idea that they needed a massive libation ceremony. They held this massive ceremony, with chiefs and dignitaries from all around in attendance, and a goat was sacrificed. After that, things ran a bit better, but not that much. Later on, when I came back to Sierra Leone and worked for a diamond company, there were a lot of other ceremonies like that taking place, and to be honest I just got used to it.

As you entered the big fenced-in area of the camp, my workshop was the first thing that you would come to. Behind me was the power station, and then the machine shop and the heavy vehicles area were further down, after which you came to the edge of the lake, where the dredge was being built. At the gates, we had a mini medical centre. It consisted of a waiting area, which was outside and was always full of local Africans. There was no other hospital for miles around, so it was busy every day, including with women having babies. When you entered through the door of the centre, there was the clinic area and beds. At the back was the doctor's room belonging to Dr Mahoi, who was a Krio who had trained in the USA. He was a nice bloke.

One day, I was coming back from lunch and saw an enormous crowd of Africans at the gates. There were normally quite a few people waiting around the clinic, but this gathering was much larger. As mentioned, my workshop was the first building through the gates, and straight away I went in there and asked the guys, "What the heck is going on out there?"

They replied, "The local police have caught these baboon men."

I had grown up reading Tarzan books and seeing the films, so I knew that leopard men were very bad, but they had to explain to me about baboon men. They were also very bad people. They would wear skins and made gloves out of iron, which had big hooks like claws. They would catch people at night, kill them, eat them and make magic potions from them, especially children and babies. They were very nasty, terrible people, and the local people were terrified of them. Later in my time in Sierra Leone, I found that if there were any reports of baboon men in the area, the guys would not work any overtime, because they wanted to walk home all together in a big group for safety. If we had a big job on which needed to be done, I would have to get a vehicle and take them home in that to make sure they got there safely, otherwise they just would not work. This particular day, the police had caught this gang of three baboon men, but they had no transport to get them to Freetown for trial and hanging. They had come to us to borrow a Land Rover! I did not see the baboon men, but they would just have looked like ordinary Africans at that point; they would have taken off the skins and gloves. That was my first introduction to the witchcraft and juju which was very prevalent in the country. I saw a lot of it in Sierra Leone.

Quite early during my time there, Taylor Woodrow wanted to arrange a football match between themselves and us at Rutile. One Saturday morning, I went down to where the dredge was to look on the noticeboard for the team sheet. I planned to write down the names of the Taylor Woodrow guys who would be playing and then ask our guys if they knew who out of them were good players. As I was writing the names down, all the local Africans gathered around me and asked what I was doing.

I said, "I'm putting a juju on your players. When this guy takes a shot, it will always go wide. Don't worry about it, you have lost the match already."

I was just joking with them, obviously, being flippant. Anyway, we played the match and Rutile won 4-0; Taylor Woodrow did not get a look-in. They wanted a rematch, and we agreed to it. The nets in the goals were made of chicken wire, as normal netting would quickly rot in the wet and the heat there. As we were walking onto the pitch for the rematch, I could see some Africans tying something into the back of the net. I shouted out to them to ask what they were doing, and they ran away. They were putting juju there: things with bits of rawhide and feathers and all sorts attached. I got it down and jumped and stamped on it. We won again!

Belief in this stuff was such a big part of the culture there. Each of the surrounding villages always had a chief. Most villages would also have a big central square, say 20ft by 20ft, with little walls all around and a roof over the top. That would be the public meeting place. The chief would be like a head of the court, and people would bring forward any concerns they had, such as that a goat had eaten somebody's plants, or a dog had stolen a chicken. They would have this once a month or so. The chief would change every year. One particular year, the chief in the local village was a guy who was from a different tribe. I met him a couple of times, and he was a lovely big guy, very well-spoken and really nice. He had only been chief for a short while when he and some of his friends were walking towards another village along a small path about two feet wide. All of a sudden, a swarm of killer bees flew down on him. One of his friends started trying to swat them off, but the bees began stinging him badly, so he ran away, as did the others. The bees stung the chief to death. The village elders obviously did not like this guy being from another tribe and had put a juju on him. How they did it, I have no idea. They must have put something on his clothing or on something he was carrying. The bees went straight for the chief and left the others alone.

When Taylor Woodrow left, we tried to get all their best workers to come over to Rutile. They had some really good guys, as well as a lot of rubbish, and I grabbed quite a few of their guys to come and work in my workshop. As I said, at this time I had two teams of 15 Africans working under me, one team on the dredge and the other in the workshop. I took one of the junior foremen down into the dredge, while the general foreman and Young Joe, the assistant foreman, continued running the workshop. One of the Africans I recruited from Taylor Woodrow was a young man from Senegal. The Senegalese are French speaking, but he could also speak and understand English OK. Believe it or not, he had also served an apprenticeship in plating and fabrication, so he could follow a proper drawing. The only way I could get him to stay with the company was to make him an assistant foreman and give him more money accordingly. Honestly, he was a boon for me. I could give him any job, big or small, and he could make it correctly. That took a lot of weight off my shoulders, leaving me free to deal with the problems that occurred on the dredge. One day, when he had been with us for a few weeks, I went to stock up on my malaria tablets at the doctor's. As I was walking through the clinic, I noticed this Senegalese man lying on a trolley bed. He looked as if he was in a coma, and his face was grey. This was not good. I knocked on the door and went in to see Dr Mahoi. As I received my tablets, I casually asked what was wrong with the young man.

All he said was, "I don't know. He was like that when they brought him in yesterday."

That told me that there was witchcraft involved about which the doctor did not want to tell me, and he probably did not know what to do. This was serious. I went straight back to the workshop and called over Young Joe.

I said, "After work, stay behind. I need you to wait for me, because I want to show you a job."

After I had finished my tasks for the day, I grabbed a Land Rover, then called in at the workshop and told Young Joe to jump in. I drove us out to a pump station that we had up on the hills, about six miles away. It was another massive man-made lake, from which we could pump water if we were ever running out down at the dredge and surrounding camp. This place was very peaceful. All there was were birds twittering away and the odd monkey making an appearance. I had been up there many times to chill just for half an hour when work was stressing me out. It was beautiful.

When Young Joe and I got there, I sat him down and said, "Now, if you don't tell me the truth of what has happened to this Senegalese lad, I am going to leave you here."

Of course, he then immediately told me the whole story. Joe Moody, the foreman, was so jealous of the Senegalese lad that he had bought a juju and put it somewhere he was working. We went back down to the workshop and searched high a low around the workbench and tools. Eventually we found it. It was a little leather pouch.

I then said, "Right, Joe, what do we do now?"

He replied, "Boss, we have to burn it." We got a fire going and burnt it. I asked Young Joe if that was it, and he said, "Yes, don't tell anybody."

It worked. I didn't even bother talking to the doctor about it again, as, being a Krio, I didn't think he would know about it anyway.

After about a month, the Senegalese lad, who was really ill and still off work, came to see me. He had recovered, but he was really thin and had lost a lot of weight.

He said, "I'm sorry, I'm going to have to leave, because the next time the foreman will kill me."

It is hard to understand how it worked. I know it is often a lot to do with suggestion, but this lad did not know there was a juju there. He only found out later when people told him about the juju. He knew he was a marked man then and would have to leave.

After Taylor Woodrow left, we kept our football team together. It was a mix of white Europeans and some Africans who worked on the mine. We used to play games away in the bush against all these other towns. We would travel a long way to play a game, and when we got there, there would be hundreds and hundreds of villagers who had come to watch. Of course, they didn't have tellies or anything, so it was entertainment for them. The pitches we played on were always very rough, and the grass was really tough. At one particular match (I played as keeper in these games), all the spectators started screaming and shouting and pointing. A snake had popped its head up in the goals. Well, they all ran in with sticks and stones and battered it to death. Then we could carry on with the game!

When I played in goal at school, I used to mark a centre on the six-yard line to help me with the angles. On these African pitches, I couldn't see the penalty spot or any lines; we didn't have a clue where anything was really, so I would find something bright and put it down to help me. In the second half of one match, we were winning 4-0, and I had gone to the edge of the area to collect the ball. I kicked it out and suddenly heard the crowd all shouting behind me. I turned around and this one lad was running off the pitch with my bit of bright paper that I had laid down as my marker. They were shouting, "We've got his juju!" I shouted at this lad, and he dropped the paper and ran into the crowd. I retrieved the paper and put it back down again. Not long after, I had to go to the edge of the area to collect the ball again. As I booted it, the same thing happened again. This time, I could not catch the little bastard, so I just had to carry on without my marker. This was not good. The next thing I knew, the ball was in the back of the net – 4-1.

A few minutes later, boom, 4-2. I had to stop this. Luckily, I managed to find another bit of paper. I made a bit of a show of showing it to the crowd, pointing and putting 'magic' on it, then I put it down, further out, towards the end of the area. They didn't score again, and we ended up winning 6-2!

In another game, we were playing a team from the banks of Sierra Leone. These lads were all young Krios and dressed really smartly before the game. The game was going our way, no problem, and towards the end of the match we were winning 4-0. Our opponents then got a penalty; luckily, I went the right way and parried it away. What happened next was a mystery to me. I was on the ground after saving the penalty, and all the African spectators just ran onto the pitch, hundreds of them. It took about 10 minutes to get them off. They were screaming, shouting and jeering constantly. I did not have a clue what was going on. When we had cleared the pitch, the referee put the ball on the spot again for another penalty. Well, that was weird. I obviously didn't want this player to have a second chance at scoring, so I walked up to him and jokingly said, "I'm sorry, pal, but you'll never score today. I'd go home if I were you." I went back to the goal, and he shot it more or less straight at me. I caught the ball and booted it out. Not long after, the whistle went. As we were walking off, I was still wondering why the referee had given a retake. I grabbed a couple of our players and asked them. They said, "When you saved it, one of the lads from behind the goals ran on and booted the ball away so the opposition couldn't score from a rebound, and then the whole crowd ran on cheering and screaming." Afterwards, both teams had a beautiful dinner together. I started to have a bit of banter with the lads from the bank, as you do, saying that they were rubbish players and so on, but all just joking. One of these lads then said, "Mr North, when you come and play us on our ground, then we will have a juju, not you." Well, that blew me away and made me think. I didn't believe that as educated people they would put stock in magic.

We used to get quite a few Americans coming out from Bethlehem Steel to the plant. They were always process specialists. We used to get quite friendly with them. They would often sit round with us and join in a singsong, and one guy, Dennis, even brought a guitar with him. We clicked immediately and enjoyed the same types of songs. After work, we would make the most of our time by jamming and singing together. We used to have some great times.

If someone new had come over from America, I used to meet them on their first night in the mess and would often say, "I'll pick you up tomorrow morning [Sunday] and take you around some of the villages." One particular guy, as we drove to a village, said to me, "Pinch me. Am I dreaming?" He was gobsmacked, seeing all these people in native dress living in little thatched mud huts. He couldn't believe it.

Every time anyone left to go back to America, they would always give me their address and say, "If you ever want to visit the States, look me up." This was a regular thing.

Around 1976, I made my first visit to the USA, which was due to Dennis. We used to get six weeks' leave in one block. On one of these periods of leave, I got back to England and decided I was going to phone Dennis and see if I could go out there. I phoned him and asked if he would mind if I visited him. He said, "Of course not!" Laker Airways was running cheap flights to the States at the time: just £37 each way. I jumped on a flight and arranged with Dennis that he would meet me at JFK airport. My flight was delayed leaving England, and then, just before we landed in JFK, the crew were calling out names of people who had messages. They called out the name North, so I went up to collect the message. It turned out it wasn't for me, so I sat back down. While waiting to go through passport control, there were quite a few people queuing. I was standing there with my suitcase and my passport ready in my hand. I was tapped on the shoulder by a gentleman from a neighbouring queue who had seen my name on my passport. He said, "My name's North, and I'm from New Zealand, but all my ancestors come from Yorkshire." Before he could say any more, I was called up to the desk. When I got through passport control, I waited for quite a while but never saw him again. I went on through to the arrivals lounge and was met by Dennis and his wife. When we got outside, it was a beautiful sunny day, and I saw all the big American cars going past. I felt as if I was home; it was such a strange feeling, but I felt as if I belonged there. On the journey from the airport into Manhattan island, the sight of all the skyscrapers just blew me away. I mean, I had been in the African bush for years! They took me up the Empire State Building, and it was amazing to see helicopters flying below and the cars down on the street looking like little Dinky toys.

Dennis lived in Pennsylvania, so we headed back there in a car journey of a few hours. They lived in a place just outside Bethlehem called Lehigh. They had a beautiful home and two special cars, a Bradley GT special kit car and a 1960 Corvette. The house was about three or four storeys high and full of antiques and pictures. They took me to the Bethlehem Steel Corporation headquarters, which was in a massive building that had shops and its own restaurant.

One of the best things that happened there was that, on a Tuesday, Dennis's wife and her father said that there was a car boot sale (which they called a swap meet). Honestly, it was massive. I could not believe how full of people it was, especially on a Tuesday. Doesn't anybody work in this area? One of the big stalls was full of musical instruments, guitars, fiddles, banjos, mandolins etc. They had everything you could think of. I zoomed in on this stall straight away and spotted a dobro, which is a type of guitar with a steel bell plate to amplify the sound. I asked how much it was, and the man said, "Sorry, that's mine." With that, he picked it up and started playing. His mate also picked up a guitar and joined in. Then they began to sing country songs. Well, the crowd just gathered around, hundreds of people. Everybody started to join in the singing. Then one of the men from the crowd joined in on a fiddle. It was unbelievable. This went on for about an hour, with them working through a repertoire of songs they knew. When they stopped playing, the crowd gave a big cheer and then started to disappear. Where would you get something like that happening back in England? For me, it was just unreal. After my visit, I flew back to England for another short while before heading back to Sierra Leone again.

    At one stage, the managing director of the company came over from the USA. Rumour had it that he was a millionaire, but he was so tight that it was unreal. It was said that, back home in Bethlehem, Pennsylvania, he didn't even have a telly. If his wife wanted to watch a particular programme, she would have to go around the corner to an old folks' home and watch it there. When Dave's replacement had arrived, the MD had met him at the airport and driven him down to the camp. The shop was only open on Friday evenings for an hour or so, and, this being a Saturday, it was closed. The MD took the new engineer to the shop and said, "You're dining with me and my wife tonight, so pick out whatever you would like." Of course, he got steaks and everything else that went with it and a bottle of wine or two. They had a really good meal. On Monday morning, when he went into his new office, the bill for the food was on his desk!

People also used to say that if the MD ever had anyone over to visit him at his house, he would let them have two beers and no more. At one stage, we had these two roofers come out to the camp, George and Bill, who stayed for about six months to put false roofs on the houses to make it less hot inside. It was Christmastime, and on Christmas Day I had the idea of gathering up things we did not need – pencils, sharpeners, rubbers etc. – and wrapping them up in newspaper (we didn't have proper wrapping paper). We then went around the houses on the camp, knocking on people's doors and wishing them a happy Christmas. When we said we had a present for them, we would be invited inside for a drink. We would then make to leave to go to another house, and the people we had visited would come with us, so the group kept growing. Finally, we got to the MD's house. By this time, there were about 20 or 30 people in our group. We were all invited in, and he did live up to his reputation and limit us to two beers each!

He might have been tight, but the MD was also very clever and sneaky. Every Saturday morning, he would come to inspect all the workshops. Everything had to be spick and span. He took notice of everything in the workshops, and if he spotted anything unusual, he wouldn't say anything about it at that point; he would retreat back to his den and read up about it. Then, he would come back the following week and ask questions to try to catch you out. You had to be on your toes all the time. Luckily, the other supervisors had warned me about him when I had first arrived and how he used to try to belittle you.

When I first took over the workshop, there were all kinds of broken and unused things lying around. One of them was a large casting of a big gear wheel, which was cracked in quite a few places. I soon realised that sooner or later the MD would notice it, read up on how to repair castings and ask me outright what I would do with it to check my knowledge. Then he would try to belittle me about it and show off superior knowledge. I didn't have a clue how to do it, so I found a book on casting repairs so that I would be prepared on his next visit. After checking everything in the workshop, the MD called me over to the casting and said, "How would you go about fixing this?" I explained that I would V-out each crack with a grinder so that I could get a nice weld in there, and I would then lay it in a bed of sand and heat up the whole casting with the massive heating nozzle that we had before I started welding. I understood that it was important to heat the whole casting, not just the parts that needed repairing, otherwise the whole thing could break very easily. I didn't have any stick welding rods; instead, I would have to use gas welding. When it was all done, I would cover it all with sand and let it cool, which would take a couple of days. Then I would turn it over and repeat the same procedure on the other side. Well, when I explained this to him, he was deflated. Not long after that, the machine shop supervisor came over and told me that they would require that casting if I could possibly repair it. I said, "Certainly!" and it worked a treat. He never tried to catch me out again after that!

One weekend, we had a visit from the prime minister, Siaka Stevens, and all his ministers. Siaka Stevens flew up in his very small mini helicopter, but all his ministers came up in a convoy of eight or nine Mercedes. In the centre of our camp was an area that was saved for all the dignitaries from the United States when they came over. There were quite a few houses there. The politicians were going to be visiting our mine and Sieromco before heading back. We didn't see Stevens, but we did see some of the ministers floating around. When they left on the Sunday, and the ministers drove off in their cars, we found that the houses had been emptied. Anything that had not been screwed down or was too big to fit into the cars had been taken: curtains, cushions, crockery, cooking pans, dishes, cutlery, stools, bedding etc. It was like a herd of human locusts had been through the houses and left them bare. These were government ministers for goodness sake! It is hard to comprehend. Luckily, the guy who ran the stores had enough to go back into at least some of the houses.

As I mentioned, at the market in Freetown, you could buy almost anything. I used to buy jeans and T-shirts there. Believe it or not, these were the goods sent by Oxfam for free. The ministers would get them and then sell them on to the market traders, who in turn sold them on to us. It was all just so corrupt it was unreal. It was terrible. As soon as the ship container came in, the goods went straight to the ministers, who made money out of them. It was a rude awakening to me; the country was just so rife with corruption. If you needed or wanted anything, you could certainly bribe your way to whatever it was.

Another job for me started when one of the engineers

came over to me from one of the other workshops to talk to me about maintaining the rollers for the D8s and D6s, the big Caterpillar diggers. There would be seven or eight of these vehicles on the site. They would be there for years, and the rollers would wear out or break. Ordering anything new would require a wait of up to six months to be delivered, which I knew, because I used to have to order simple tools, French chalk, welding rods etc. I had to make sure we had plenty of welding rods of every size and description in constant supply, from mild steel to hard facing rods. There was a lot of maintenance required by all of the mining equipment we had on site.

The top rollers on these vehicles are called jockey rollers, and then there are other rollers on the bottom. There could be up to five rollers on the bottom depending on the size of the vehicle, and two rollers on the top. As I have said, you couldn't go out and buy new ones in the middle of Africa, so we had to keep the ones we had repaired. We had an old lathe in the workshop, and this engineer wanted me to convert the lathe, put the rollers in the chuck, put it on a low speed and build up the rollers with the stick rods. I had worked on lathes when I had worked for my dad, as he had quite a few of them. I knew you could never run them slow enough to do what the engineer was asking; the welder wouldn't be able to do his job and control the lathe at the same time.

When I first arrived at Sierra Rutile, I had been looking around one day and had found a storeroom with bits of old equipment in it. This storeroom belonged to the previous company who had operated the screw dredge on the site. I went back through the contents of the storeroom and had a really good look at this strange kind of welding machine that I found there. It had a chuck for holding things like wheels and also foot pedals and all sorts, but I was sure that I could make it work somehow. I found a manual with it and realised that the machine had never been touched and was just lying there. There were also rolls and rolls of flux core wire with it, which I had never heard of at that stage. It was all hard-facing wire. How it works is that the shielded flux is inside the core, which shields it from impurities. It is clever stuff that lays down a very hard surface, mainly used in mining to build up worn wheels, tips on the big buckets of D8s and D6s etc. and lasts a heck of a lot longer than ordinary mild steel would. We also used it on the dredge buckets later on. I looked at the machine and could see that that was what it was for and why it had been brought out there by the previous company. To me, it was a bonus. I took the machine into the workshop, fastened it to the lathe bed and began to try it out. I now had a solution that meant I could put the rollers in the chuck and control the speed of both the chuck and the flux core wire. The welder had a foot pedal to stop and start it, and they could set the speed. It worked brilliantly and was made for the job. We could now repair the rollers like crazy. When the engineer came to see what we were doing, he chewed me out for not using the lathe. He was really upset! Some people! I knew his lathe idea was impractical and my solution was better. Nobody had noticed this great machine just lying there going to rust. This was just another example of an engineer who lacked practical experience.

At one point, I got friendly with a new couple who had just come out, Jeff and Beverly. They had been working in Zambia on the copper belt, where I had been. He had been working in Mufulira, one of the other towns north of

Luanshya. I told them where I had worked, and Bev said, "I don't remember your name. I grew up in Luanshya." I had to tell her that nobody remembered my real name, as everybody had called me Ringo. She replied, "My God, my girlfriends and I used to rush up to the mine complex just to see you drive up on your motorbike. We were all about 11 or 12 at the time!" Fame again!

Beverly had grown up in Africa, and she loved animals. If anybody had an injured pet, they would take it to her. One day, they found a big hawk which had got caught in a fence. She nursed it back to health until it flew away, recovered. They always had a monkey or a mongoose as a pet. Even I had a mongoose as a pet for a while. They are very inquisitive and funny. If anybody came into the house, it would come over to check them out straight away. One day, I invited some of the African workers over for a couple of beers at my house. They came all dressed up in shirts and long pants. Well, this mongoose ran up the first guy's trouser leg. He was hopping around and screaming. I had forgotten to warn them about my mongoose! After a while, maybe a few months, the animal would just go away, probably off looking for a mate.

One day, Bev went into her kitchen, and there was this big snake on the worktop. Well, she screamed, and the houseboy ran in holding the mongoose. He threw the mongoose onto the worktop beside the snake. Bev was there watching, and all she could see was a blur of fur and flesh. There was blood and bits flying off everywhere. She panicked that much that when she got the chance, she grabbed the mongoose's tail and pulled it away. Then the snake pounced and bit the mongoose. When they looked, it was the snake that was all bitten and mauled. The snake was the one getting a real pounding from the mongoose. The houseboy finished the snake off with a frying pan. The mongoose's leg where it had been bitten swelled up to about four times the size. Bev looked after it while the houseboy ran off into the bush looking for herbs. When he came back, they put a poultice on the leg. The mongoose took itself away and hid for about a week, and when it came back it was as right as rain.

Another amusing story from my time at Sierra Rutile is from when I found one of the Africans, James, looking very despondent one day. I went to ask him what the matter was, and his reply was that, late in the afternoon of the previous day, a hoard of monkeys had jumped down from the trees and wrecked his garden. The Africans all grew most of their own food: sweet potatoes, casavas and loads of other African vegetables. The monkeys had gone through, ripping everything up and destroying all the food. Then they had disappeared back into the trees before anyone could do anything about it. I tried to console James, not really understanding the effect this event was having on him.

Standing there so forlorn, he turned to me and said, "Mr North, what do you do about your monkeys back in England?"

I replied, "James, we don't have monkeys in England."

He said, most indignantly, "Of course you do, everyone has monkeys, they're everywhere!"

That was his view on the world.

While I was working for Rutile, I was approached by a representative of the National Diamond Company to come for an interview. It meant that I had to go down to Freetown and then out to Hastings airport in the bush. I got on a small Trislander plane, which, as I have said before, had three propellers, two on the wings and one on the tail. They were very powerful and could land and take off in small spaces. There were four rows of seats behind the pilot, who was, of course, up at the front. There were other passengers in the front row, and I chose to sit at the back. Then they took out the two middle rows of seats and stuck these two big fridges in! I didn't have any view in front of me, just to either side. When we set off, the whole journey was at treetop level. Visibility was bad, as it was the rainy season. To me, it ended up as a white-knuckle ride. All I could see were trees flashing past and the pilot dodging hills. This was a nightmare! We landed for one quick stop, during which time the front row passengers got off and some others got on. I was outside stretching my legs, and when I looked down at the wheels of the plane, I could see twigs and branches and leaves stuck in them!

We set off again and arrived at the National Diamond Company, where I got off. I was made very welcome: they fed and watered me, and I could see that it was a really nice camp. It was similar to what I was used to but with a nice clubhouse. The boss explained what his problem was and why they required me. We had a tour of the working area, and he was showing me all the problems. I soon realised what they required. They needed a mobile squad with a team and all the gear loaded onto trucks or trailers, ready to go to wherever the breakdown was.

That night in the clubhouse, I made good friends and met ex-pats like me. The pilot was there at the bar, so I went up and had a word with him, complaining about how terrible the flight was.

He said, "When we go back tomorrow, come and sit next to me; it's no problem."

Wow! I thought that was a great offer. What an experience that turned out to be. Come the next morning, I was sat next to him, and he gave me the earphones, ready to take off. He passed me a road map. I asked what it was for, and he said, "Because it's the rainy season, we can't see for all the clouds. When the visibility is bad, we can only follow the roads." I had been right the day before: he was dodging big trees and hills while trying to keep sight of the road below us! There were no wipers on the window, and when I asked him how he managed to see, he just said, "Oh, that makes it even harder."

I didn't hear back from the diamond mine, so I assumed that they had just used my idea of forming a mobile squad or come up with a better idea themselves. Maybe they found somebody else. However, I would meet up again with some of the friends I met there – more on that later.

I went back to Rutile, and by this time I had acquired an old Toyota Corolla. It had been a Freetown taxi and had been around the clock three times, with over 300,000mi. on the clock, but it still ran. The reason I had this was the tight-fisted MD. He would not allow us to use the company vehicles for private use. He used to cycle down to the site after tea and feel the vehicles' engines to see if any of them had been used. Like I said, sneaky. In due course, everybody complained about him, and we eventually got rid of him and he was replaced, but that was the kind of rule he would implement.

At one stage, there was a big agricultural show in a town called Bo, which was quite a long way away. We checked the map to find a way there without having to cross any rivers. This was towards the end of the dry season, so the rivers were low, and we knew that the ferries would stick and wouldn't be able to take us across. We set off, and it was a great weekend. Everybody and his dog were there, including devil dancers and various societies. There were singing and dancing competitions. One of the societies was called the Bundu, and they were not nice. These were the people who would take the young girls when they were coming into puberty and circumcise them – mutilate them. These girls were brainwashed as they were growing up into believing that this society would make them into a woman. Terrible.

I always felt safe at events like these, surrounded by lots of native people. People were always very friendly. However, you always had to hide your money. There would be something going on in a big hut, and, as you entered, people would be crowded tightly together. You would be able to feel people's hands going into your pockets, feeling for your wallet. It was important to have your money stashed away elsewhere, like down your socks!

On the way back, we were having a good time. I was with George, who was one of the roofers, and we were driving along in my old Corolla. We were looking for a faster route back to the camp, because it was a long journey, something like a 200mi. round trip, and we had left it a bit late. We found this route where there was just one river to cross – sounds good, eh? We pulled up at the ferry, and the people said, "Sorry, but you won't get across." By this stage, late in the afternoon, we just didn't have time to backtrack the way we had come and then drive the same route we had used on the way there. We just had to get across there.

We bribed the man and persuaded him to take us across. These ferries are actually more like rafts up on 50gal. drums, with a cable across. It could take four cars, and we put our car in the middle. There was a gang of about six guys, each with wood that looked like a club with a slot at the end, which they would hook onto the cable and pull like an oar to move us across the river. As we were going across, we grounded. We were about 50–60ft away from the bank. Oh shit! What do we do now? I found two planks, which we tried to use, but, as I drove the wheels of the car onto them, they just sank, with me on them. I ended up sitting there up to my waist in water. The engine was still running! Luckily, there was a bunch of locals on the far bank, falling about laughing. We shouted over to them to come and help push the car, which they did. We got the car off and up the steep bank, with the engine still running. I pulled the handbrake on and opened all the doors and the boot to let the water run out. We paid the locals and were able to carry on the journey! The only bad thing was that George's camera had been on the back seat and was completely ruined. The Corolla suffered no ill effects, which was amazing.

At one time, much later on, we had a Jeep. It had been raining heavily, and I was driving it through the bush one day and came to a big puddle. It's a Jeep; it'll drive through no problem. It just stopped right in the middle. With the heat, it soon dried out and I was able to drive off again, slowly. I had expected better.

One of my jobs was sourcing charcoal for our weekly barbecue nights, which we held every Friday. Every week, everyone would come to the barbecue and bring their own meat. I would get mine from the mess. One particular time, we were going to have a fancy-dress party. We bought a pig to barbecue – a hog roast. These things always came down to me – muggins – so I had to set about making a turning spit using a geared down motor and making a big tray to catch the fat and baste the pig. I had never done anything like that before, but there was lots of good advice flying around. Our pig was stuffed with garlic, apples, oranges, you name it; we put everything we could get our hands on inside this pig. It took the whole day to cook it. People would call by to see how I was doing and would bring me a beer. We would have a chat, and then they would wander off and someone else would come up. One woman was cooking a small goat in the oven, and the rest of the ladies were making different kinds of salads. There were some nice costumes. I had stuck a band around my head with a feather in it, put on just a waistcoat with no shirt and said I was a Red Indian.

The hog roast was a terrific success, and, honestly, the meat was beautiful. When we had finished serving everyone, George and I went and sat down to eat ours. Within a few minutes, people started to come up to ask for seconds. I told them just to go ahead and help themselves. They came back saying, "Where have you put the pig?" to which I replied, "It's on the bench outside the door where we were serving it." We all went out, and it was gone. We looked everywhere, but no pig. We asked people if they had seen it, but nobody had. Then I stopped one guy who was coming back from his house and said, "I'm not being funny, but have you seen our pig anywhere?"

He said, "Yeah, I saw the security guards carrying it out of the gate."

He obviously thought that we had given them permission. The swine! We didn't feel that we could chew them out about it, because they were good guys. The story came back that the pig fed some of the villagers for a week at least!

One of the main characters I remember was Mr Boli

(pronounced bowlie), who was a big American man in his 40s. When I say big, I mean big. He was about six feet two with big shoulders and a wide chest – just a massive guy, but a great guy. Everything about him was nice. At the barbecue nights, he used to bring a big dish of Boli beans. There is no comparison between our beans and American beans. The nearest explanation I could give is that if you think of the flavour of the beans you get at Kentucky Fried Chicken, it was similar. In America, you couldn't find any Heinz beans; they were all different flavours. Mr Boli used to make these spicy beans for our Friday-night barbecues, which were great. His favourite song was Simon Smith and His Amazing Dancing Bear. At any dance or party, he would always request it, and then he would become the dancing bear. He used to clear the floor, as he knocked everybody out of the way.

One Sunday morning, the houseboy came and knocked me up early and said, "Come and look at Mr Boli's house." He lived a few doors down from me. When I went out, I could see that there was dried blood everywhere: on the door, the walls, the floor. The houseboy thought that Boli had been killed. We gently opened the door and saw that he was on the bed, covered in blood. He was snoring! We gently shook him and asked, "Boli, what's wrong?"

He finally woke up, saying, "What's going on?"

When the story came out, it seemed that he had been at a party at someone's house the night before. He had gone to get more beer, and, as he was heading back, he had tripped up while carrying a load of bottles of beer, and they had smashed. He was cut all over and had just drunkenly staggered home. He couldn't remember anything about it!

Another Sunday morning, we had arranged to go out

and try to get palm wine from some of the palm trees. Palm wine is a lethal drink, believe you me. It is what the Africans drink. You just tap the tree, it runs out and you drink it. That particular morning, I was called out very early on a breakdown on the dredge, so I missed out on the adventure. I got back in the early afternoon and was dozing when Boli got back. Yes, he had found the right palm trees, tapped them and got really drunk. He came down through the cabins, banging on the doors, shouting, "Northy, you old fart, where are you? Come out!" When I came out, he was covered in sick from head to toe – what a mess! His glasses were sideways like Eric Morecambe. He then grabbed me in a bear hug – ugh! I looked in his Land Rover, and he had been leaning out the window, throwing up. I was glad I missed that trip!

He was quite a character but a super guy. When we used to get our six weeks' holiday, he would either go home to the States at the start or reach the States by the end. The rest of the time, he would travel to every country he possibly could, with the aim of drinking a beer in every country. That was his holiday!

On Sunday afternoons, we played football on the fields down the hill from where we lived. We were playing a football match one afternoon, just a friendly between ourselves. There were quite a few spectators there. The field was at the side of the road, going up towards our camp. There were telegraph poles and power lines running alongside. All of a sudden, the spectators down the roadside of the pitch all set off running up the hill. They had been attacked by killer bees. Halfway up the hill was a waterhole that the African ladies used to wash clothes in. They all dived into the water to get away from the bees! The bees must have made a nest on one of the poles.

During another match one day, the manager drove down and said they had a problem on the ship. This was the very first shipload of ore that we had produced. The ore was very heavy and fine. The ore would go down via a conveyor system into a hopper and then it would be poured into special sealed wagon compartments that prevented any moisture getting in. At the dock, the ore would be loaded into a barge with sealed covers and would then be taken by two tugs out to a cargo ship. The ships couldn't get anywhere near, as the estuary was too shallow, so it would take three or four hours to get out to the ship. They had ordered a cargo ship with rubber-lined grabs, but someone had screwed up and sent a cargo ship with ordinary grabs, which were old, warped and bent. When they had tried to pick up the ore, it had all fallen out into the sea. Oh dear. I'm glad it wasn't gold! The manager had come to the football field to tell me this and ask what we could do.

We filled a tugboat with welding plants, cutting gear, welding rods, strips of metal, everything we could think of. As I said, it took us three or four hours to get out to the ship, where they picked up all our gear and took us up to look at the grabs. They were so bent out of shape and broken, some with nearly six-inch gaps. It was a major job, and these grabs were massive. There were six grabs on one side of the ship and another six grabs on the other side. We had to send for more steel, and from leaving Rutile to coming back at the end of the job, it was three days. I didn't sleep at all. I had about 10 guys with me and split them in half, working day and night. When we had finished, we had made the grabs like new; you couldn't get a piece of paper between them. The crew and the captain were really happy with what we had achieved, and the ship's captain gave me a huge bonus of around 200 leone. I gave it to the team to share out between themselves. Mind you, as usual, when I got back to base, there were no medals or recognition. Nobody said anything about it. It took me hours under the shower scrubbing to get the ore off my skin; it was ingrained. Then I slept.

Another disaster happened not long after that, again with a cargo ship. The swell was so big that when the barge went out there, it bumped into the ship. It caused a split about 12ft long in the side of the ship, right on the waterline. We had to load welding equipment, including cutting gear and gouging nozzles, and head back out there again. We were able to stand on one of the tugboats, the back of which was at water level, and work from there. They had emptied the side of the ship with the split and put all the ore on the other side so that it was tilting over and keeping the damage just above the waterline. It had split on the band, which I had to take off. The band was an inch thick by 12in. wide. The split was 12ft long, just short of four metres. As I have said, I had done all kinds of cutting and welding in the past, so I gouged it off using a gouging torch, which is a cutting tool with a special nozzle. I couldn't cut into the metal of the ship; I could only cut the weld out. Then I had to split down either side without damaging the ship. We got it off, and, luckily, we had all kinds of metal there to work with. They had one that was very similar in size which we could use. We had to V out the split and then do multiple welds to make sure it was watertight. The barge and the ship were moving all the time, which made it even more difficult. I had picked the best welders to come with me, and these guys were really good. It took us a day and a half of working non-stop to finish the job. When we had finished it, they had to fly the harbourmaster out from Freetown to check it. He came out and inspected it at night-time under lights. If the job had been done in the harbour, it would have been X-rayed to check for impurities. The harbourmaster passed the ship with flying colours, but again no medals! I gave my lads a bonus out of my own pocket for producing such a great job. As far as I know, the ship didn't sink on the way to the States!

There are other jobs I can remember when I had to think outside the box. One was when there was a serious breakdown. There was a leak on a conveyor, which was partly underground and carried a lot of the ore slurry. It was losing a lot of liquid through the split but was in a place that made it really hard to access. There were no power points where I could plug in my stick welder or anything. I ended up dragging the bottles of oxyacetylene near, knocking all the flux off my welding rods so that they were just bare metal and welding the conveyor up with a cutting torch. The Africans were amazed and just stood there gobsmacked. They had never seen anything like that. A cutting torch is big, not like a welding torch, which has very fine nozzles. You are actually using the cutting head but not squeezing for the oxygen that blows the hole. Nobody had used a cutting torch in that way before; I was the first, I think.

One of the things we did at Sierra Rutile in the late 1970s was go on missions of mercy. There was a guy who ran the power plant for us, keeping the generators going that gave us electricity and powered the pumps and so on. He was quite a good bloke, and every couple of months he would load up a Land Rover with diesel, oil and all kinds of equipment and tools and ask us to go out with him to this hospital that was way out in the bush, about 150mi. away.

The equipment was donated by the company, and he would go out to the hospital to service their generators and all the power plants, boilers etc. to keep the place running. The hospital was run by Irish nuns. The lady who ran the whole shooting match was in her 60s or 70s, and she was also the chief surgeon doing all the operations. She was a Mother Teresa-like figure. Other nurses would fly out from Ireland to work there, and they were on very little pay, just a pittance. It used to make us feel so humble, being there to help these people. The hospital was massive but was funded just by donations from their order, as I doubt they charged the Africans for any of the treatment they gave them. Now and again, the chief surgeon would come back with us to Rutile for a curry Sunday and bring a couple of her helpers with her, which was quite nice.

Like us, after a while, they would let some of the nurses go down to Freetown for R & R. On one of their trips, one of the nurses was swimming and got caught in a rough swell. She ended up with a broken leg. They just put her back in the Land Rover and drove her back to the hospital to get her sorted. Think about it. What a horrible journey for that poor girl. Half the roads were just rough dirt with potholes. That girl must have gone through one painful journey, bumping along a couple of hundred miles back into the bush.

I had been working for Sierra Rutile for about three years before Ron Finger arrived as my boss. By this stage, most of my time was spent on the dredge, because there were that many problems down there. They had got some people in to run the workshop in my place. The American system is that anything to do with welding or fabrication or metalwork means that your job title is classed as 'welder'. The advert to which I had responded was for a welder. In England, that's not the case; the job title of welder literally means that you can do welding. As a result, the lads that turned up there for jobs that involved more complete fabrication often had no experience of it at all, and it was hard for them.

To illustrate what I mean, years later, when I was back in England, I had a job as a foreman in a small fabrication shop. They weren't paying me much, and I soon got another job paying me £1 an hour more somewhere else. When I handed in my notice, the boss said, "What am I going to do? I need a foreman." I told him I had just the lad for him. In one of the other places at which I had worked, I had been general foreman of a company that made petrol tanks for wagons and things like that. The operation was split into three shifts, and they had a foreman on each shift. I was the general foreman looking after the whole workshop. I met one of the young lads I knew from there (one of the shift foremen) and told him that I knew of a place looking for a foreman. He was a good bloke, and he got the job, but he only lasted three weeks. He couldn't handle it and just quit. He had been a fabricator, doing small jobs, and when he moved up to bigger-scale, more complicated jobs, it was an entirely different ball game.

Ron came out to Sierra Leone with his family. He brought his wife, Paulette, and two children, both about seven years old. The boy was Big Ron's son, and the girl was Paulette's daughter. You would never have guessed they had different parents; they both had blond hair, as had Paulette, and Ron's was sandy coloured. He was originally from Boise in Idaho, where his dad was a big boss in a company out there. Ron and I were of a similar age. We clicked and got on really well. He had degrees in welding engineering, electrical engineering and mining engineering. He was a clever bloke, and I never knew him to be beaten by anything. He could fix anything, believe you me. He had a general knowledge of everything.

Big Ron was about six feet five and the strongest man I have ever met. Chain blocks are sort of gears with chains hanging down. Then there would be a hook. You hang the chain block up, and if you are lifting something, you pull the chains. It is like a big metal pulley-type system. They can be very heavy, and to carry them you would hold the block in one hand and all the wrapped-up chains in the other hand to balance yourself. Two Africans saw Ron carrying one of the heaviest chain blocks one day and said that they would move it for him. He passed the block to one of them and the chains to the other. They both fell flat on the ground with the weight!

Ron lived in one of the nice houses on the site, and the family had brought an organ with them. As far as I know, Ron had met Paulette in Vegas, where she had performed as part of a duo in the lounge bars there. She was a nice singer and played the keyboard. We used to have a lot of musical evenings at their house, playing every song we knew, with Paulette playing the organ and me on guitar. One song that I think upset Ron was Big Boss Man, which I think Elvis sang at one time. The words go: 'You ain't so big; you're just tall, that's all.' I didn't realise the significance of it until quite a few years later, when I realised that I must have pissed him off singing that.

Once, I asked Ron if he had ever thought about learning karate. He told me a story in reply. He had been in a bar one night and some guy was mouthing off about a karate competition he had just won. It was a major competition, and there had been big posters on the wall advertising it the day before. Finally, Ron had had enough, and when this guy got stroppy, Ron punched him spark out. He said, "I realised I didn't need to learn karate after that!"

As I have mentioned, we had a good centre in the Rutile camp, with a 10-pin bowling alley and pool tables. One night, Ron and I went down to play pool, and he pulled out this beautiful case. It was all ivory with what looked like gold inlay. This was the 1970s, and I had never seen anything like it; it was unbelievable. I had also never seen a jointed pool cue before. I asked, "Where did you get that from?" He replied that, being in construction work in the States, he had worked all over the country. One night, he had been playing pool in a bar that had a couple of tables. There were quite a few other people playing, and, after a while, trouble started. In the States, they always play for money. A few younger lads started giving trouble to this old guy. Of course, Ron joined in to help the old guy. They were up against quite a number of the locals, and Ron started laying about with his cue, which he broke over somebody's head. They managed to get out in one piece, and as he and the old guy were heading over to their cars, Ron said, "The worst thing about that fight was that my favourite cue is broken." The old man then opened his boot and gave him this beautiful case. Ron was gobsmacked. As the old guy got into his car, he said, "Thanks anyway. My name is Minnesota Fats." He was a famous pool shark. His character was in the film The Hustler with Paul Newman (Jackie Gleason played Minnesota Fats).

It was coming up to 5th November, and as a lot of people on the site were from England, we made a bonfire. We had a barbecue and a competition for the children to make the best guy. There were about five or six children involved, plus Ron's two. I had to explain to Ron what a guy was: you get a dummy and clothe it. The general manager's wife would pick out the best one. Of course, she declared that they were all good and they all got sweets and a present. After the fire was lit and burning well, we threw all the guys onto it. Well, Ron started shouting, "What are you doing?!" It was then that we found out that he had put his son's best clothes on the dummy. They didn't know that they were going to be burnt! Obviously, it was too late, as the guys were burning fiercely. Both Ron and Paulette asked why we had thrown them on the fire, not understanding about Guy Fawkes. Boy, did I have some explaining to do! They still didn't understand the barbaric concept. When you think about it, Guy Fawkes wasn't burnt; he was sentenced to be hung, drawn and quartered. There were four of them in the plot, and they were all tortured very badly. Guy Fawkes watched the other three be hung and split open and must have thought he didn't need that, because, after climbing onto it, he jumped off the platform, which broke his neck, and he died instantly. Mind you, they still cut him open and into quarters, but he didn't have to undergo the disembowelling while alive. Days before the execution, which was in January 1606, Parliament passed the Observance of 5th November Act, which made it compulsory to celebrate Bonfire Night or Guy Fawkes Night. That's why we still celebrate it today. The bonfire and the fireworks seem more like celebrating the intended explosion.

At Christmastime, we were having a party, and all the Africans from the dredge and the workshop came along. We bought a couple of cases of beer for them and were having a good party together. The Africans are proud of their bodies. Half of them don't wear any tops, and, in terms of bodyweight, there is no fat on them at all. Halfway through the party, they decided they wanted to have an arm-wrestling competition. There were about 30 of them all standing there in a queue, while one by one Ron just pushed their arms over with no effort at all. More people joined the queue to have a go. By the time he had beaten about 45 opponents, Ron was getting a bit slower. I could see he was getting a bit tired, and I whispered, "Ron, I think you had better just quit. If one of these guys ever beat you, he'll be a king and never stop bragging!" He took my advice and stopped.

After a while, Paulette and the kids went back to the States, but Ron stayed on in Sierra Leone for some time longer. Eventually, he got so frustrated with the management and the way they were trying to run things that he just packed up. The leadership were lacking in experience, whereas Ron had a lot of construction and mining experience, so he knew what he was doing. However, the management just wouldn't listen to us. While in Freetown, Ron was offered a job by the casino owner there, going to look for gold and diamonds for him. This casino owner, we found out later, was another big rogue. He was a Krio and used to be a high court judge. This man was evil. At one time, he bought a ship full of booze from Italy – all the best wines, whiskies and liqueurs. When the ship arrived in Freetown harbour, he sent for the whole crew to come ashore that night for a celebration with him. He also sent a gang out to empty the ship of all the goods, then open all the valves and sink the ship. He then claimed on the insurance for the lot! Very crafty. The Italian company sent out two investigators, who I think were divers. They went down and found that the ship had all the valves open and came back to report it to the casino owner. He had them escorted back to the plane with the instruction, "Leave or die; it's your choice."

While a high court judge, he threw out of court the evidence about a big diamond robbery, letting off everyone who had been charged with the crime. He then retired as a very rich man. Very suspicious. The robbery had happened in 1969 at Hastings airport, which was about an hour away from Freetown, in the bush. A gang of Africans had surrounded a plane, beaten up the guards, taken a box containing a month's worth of diamonds (over $3.5 million) and driven off into Freetown. It was very well planned, as, don't forget, there were no phones at that time in Sierra Leone. The version of the story I heard was that the gang of Africans who had committed the crime were then going around the bars in Freetown, bragging about what they had done and spending money like water. The police rounded them up, but of course there were no diamonds found in their possession. The case went to court, but, as I say, it was then thrown out by the man who had now offered Ron a job.

Ron accepted the job, and I managed to smuggle him some tools from Rutile. I filled a big toolbox and sent one of my good lads, Sammy Bangura, to give it to Ron. I then realised that it was time for me to leave Rutile too. I told the management that I was leaving and served my notice. On the day that I was packing to leave, representatives from Sieromco, the nearby bauxite mine, arrived. They asked if I would take over as the washing plant supervisor there. Obviously, they had heard that I was leaving Rutile, and their supervisor had been flown back to Switzerland, suffering from Lassa fever. Five thousand people a year die from Lassa fever around the west coast of Africa, so I knew it was very serious. I told them that I would think about it and decide when I got down to Freetown. Sieromco mined about 700,000 tonnes of bauxite a year and then shipped it back to Switzerland. It was an open cast mine, and the washing plant was the main plant where the ore was crushed, washed, put onto conveyors and then transferred into hoppers for shipping.

I arrived in Freetown, and Rutile put me up in the company digs there. I planned to get a taxi out to where the restaurants were on the beach and have a good meal that evening. By pure luck, as I was passing by the casino on the same beach road for hotels etc., Ron came out. He had lost a lot of weight and was in such a bad way that he could barely stand. I took him with me for a meal, and over dinner he told me his story. As a former judge, the casino owner was a very articulate and persuasive man and had convinced Ron to take the job with him, but it had all gone wrong since I had last seen him. He had been left high and dry without money and couldn't get the drugs to treat the malaria from which he had been suffering. One night, when he was becoming ill and was delirious, Ron was staying in this small hut on site. Suddenly, the window of the hut had flown open, Ron had jumped out of bed and all he had been able to see were these two big eyes staring at him through the window. Ron hit this thing and immediately heard a big scream. He ran outside, and there was this goat laid on its back with all four legs in the air, spark out unconscious! The owner tried to sue Ron, but he was having none of it.

Ron had now come back from the site to ask the casino owner for money and a ticket home, but he had been refused. Running true to form, he wouldn't even give Ron the time of day. Previous to this, I had met a young lad who also worked for this casino owner, catching tropical fish, which were then shipped out for sale. When I met him, this lad was also in a desperate state and not being paid, so it was obviously something he did a lot: take and take and never give.

I took Ron back to where I was staying, and the next morning we went to the airplane booking office, where I handed him my ticket home and asked them to exchange it for one going to the States. They eventually did this, changing the destination from London to New York. I headed to the Sieromco office, where I told them that I would take the job at the washing plant and would travel up there as soon as I could. I stayed with Ron until he flew out and in-between times sent a telegram to my mum saying that I was sorry but I had accepted another job for a further six months or so.

Ron later told me that he had brought a couple of diamonds down to Freetown with him as a kind of insurance in case the casino owner wouldn't cough up. Once he was in New York, he was able to get a good price for the two diamonds that he had smuggled out. That got him back to his home in Oregon and paid off some of his bills. He later paid me back for the plane ticket, got the medication he needed and began to recover. It was at this stage that Ron was contacted by a millionaire whose son ran a gold mining project in the Cave Junction area of Oregon. I guess he heard that Ron was back from Sierra Leone where he had been mining ore, gold and diamonds and thought he was the right man to front a new venture in Africa. More on that later.

I, meanwhile, went to Sieromco, where I already knew most of the people. That made the transition easy, but the work was very hard. Keeping all the machinery running was difficult. The conveyors would seize up, and that would be a major operation to strip out and replace sections of seized rollers. It was a continuous job. The crushing plant was the same: always new problems. A rock would jam in the machinery and everything would come to a standstill. I was under pressure all the time to keep the ore moving and make sure that the mine would meet the required weekly and monthly production quota.

Life there outside of work was much the same as Rutile. We would have musical evenings, film showings, swimming and visits to the curry Sundays at Rutile. After six months or so, the gentleman whose job I was covering had recovered and he returned. Sieromco paid me what I was due, bought my ticket and I said my goodbyes to everybody, not knowing that I would be back just a short while later.

I helped make the dredge. This was commemorated by the dredge being put on a 10-leones note. Up to then, the biggest note was a five. Each leone was roughly equal to a dollar

This was maintenance day. We were working on the pipeline

Here we are waiting to start the libation ceremony. Notice the sections of pipelines stacked up ready to use

The actual ceremony, letting the goat's blood flow into the lake

My foreman: Joe Moody, me Patrick Sheriff, Steve and Joe
(whose nickname was Young Joe)

This is the barge that carried the ore and broke the sides of the ship. No wonder

Some of the devil dancers at the bo show

Congoli, one of the devil dancers

My pet mongoose

Me and my boss boy at Sieromco

CHAPTER EIGHT
BB&S

As soon as I landed back in England in late 1980, I got in touch with Ron. He told me about a proposition to mine for gold and diamonds back in Sierra Leone. Of course, I was interested. The company was called BB&S (Bentley, Brissette & Spooner), but in Africa they wouldn't let a company be called by people's names, so there it was called Big Bent Spoon! Mr Bentley was a multimillionaire who owned a massive company called Bentley Laboratories, which made medical equipment in Irin, California. Mr Brissette was an Afro-American who had spent many years in Sierra Leone buying diamonds, which he had then taken back to the States, where he had sold them. Brissette then met Bentley, who was going to financially back the enterprise. Mr Spooner was an international attorney and president of the chamber of commerce for Newport Beach, where a lot of big businesses were located. His office was like something out of the telly show Dallas. On the wall was a picture of him being presented with something by President Eisenhower for serving 25 years in the CIA. These people were big fish!

The company had headhunted Ron, but he wouldn't agree to work with them until they took me on as well. They arranged to fly me out to the States to meet with Ron and the owners of BB&S, which was based in Orange County, California. I flew into Cave Junction, which is in the south of Oregon, near the Californian border. They put me up in a nice motel, and I then had to fly down to Orange County to meet Mr Spooner. Mr Spooner escorted me around the area and took me to see Mr Bentley (Mr Brissette was back in Africa, setting up deals). The two of them put me through a kind of interview, which I passed OK based on my experience helping build a diamond dredger while in Cape Town and then working for years in various mines. A salary of $2,600 per month was agreed, and I was then flown back to the motel in Cave Junction. The next morning, I met the millionaire's son, Jim Bentley. He was nothing like his father. To me, he must have been the black sheep of the family, and I was not impressed. He and some others were running a gold mining enterprise in the area around Cave Junction. I don't know whether it was successful or not.

While I had been working for Sieromco, Ron, now fully recovered, had been buying the equipment we would need, including a collection of semi-trucks and trailers. One of the main pieces was a massive purpose-built trailer to be used as a gold and diamond screening plant. It was a really complicated piece of equipment and had big water cannons on it designed for washing and sorting rocks. Later, I would have a smaller version built to help with our operations. Ron had even got us a refrigerated truck in which we could live and control the temperature. Ron and I went to a big tool shop and more or less bought the place out, including six months' worth of dried food, welding plants and every tool you can think of. We had enough to fill 12 trucks. It would have been amazing if it had worked out.

A couple of days after my meeting with the company owners in Orange County, I started to suffer a flare up of malaria. This time it was really bad. My tablets were in my suitcase, which had gone AWOL in transit, and I was shaking and vomiting terribly for days. Bentley Junior called to see me, and it scared him to death when he saw the state I was in. When I first met him, he had been busy telling me that he owned a ranch, and he used to do all the operations on the animals there, making out he was such a hard man, yet the sight of me with malaria really frightened him. I said that he had to take me to the closest hospital, because by now I had this terrible headache too. I was dehydrated, and my tongue seemed to have swollen up in my mouth. We got into his vehicle and set off, but I had to get him to stop at a shop by the road so that I could get a drink and boiled sweets for me to suck, which helped a bit. I got to the hospital, where they gave me medication and they got me back to somewhere near normal. That was the worst I had ever been with malaria, and I think I was close to getting cerebral malaria, from which I don't think you ever really recover.

When I was better, I then flew out to Sierra Leone, where I again met with Mr Spooner and with Mr Brissette. We stayed in the Cape Sierra Hotel on the beach. The beach was half an hour journey from Freetown and had a few hotels and restaurants along the beachfront. Mr Spooner told me that he had just had a full medical examination and was 100% approved to fly out to Africa. We had been given $1 million up front, which had supposedly been deposited in the Bank of Sierra Leone, and I started to gather together men and vehicles. Mr Brissette had already acquired a Volkswagen Kombi and a couple of drivers. Ron, meanwhile, was getting the equipment to Galveston in Texas, the port from where it would be shipped out to Africa. My first job was to acquire a place to store it all once it had been offloaded and then to find a way that we could get it to an area called Lake Sonfon. This was in the mountains and was a lake where sacrifices and all sorts of libation ceremonies had taken place. Lots of gold had been put into the lake to please the gods and devils. It was about 230mi. from Freetown, and the proper roads finished approximately 100mi. away from the area to which we had to get. From what I can remember, we had five sets of semi-trucks and trailers, and there were a lot of rivers and streams to cross on the way there – not an easy task!

The lake itself was very strange: it was on a plateau on top of a mountain and took ages to get to. It was near to the end of the dry season when I got there, so there was no water in this lake, just reeds and trees and bushes growing in it. To me, it looked like a meteor had crashed into the earth there, like a perfectly round bed of melted rock.

While waiting for the ship to arrive, we started mining at quite a few sites using primitive methods like head pans and shovels. All the sites had been previously selected by mining geologists called Michael and George. If all the equipment arrived and was put to use, the estimates from their samples indicated that we would have had a great operation. Until the point when we were granted our own mining licences, which could take up to two years, we would have to take on local partners. They would rent the area, which we couldn't legally do. From whatever money the operation made, we were allowed to deduct the costs we had incurred in getting to the diamonds, and then the remaining profit would be split 50:50.

The company had chosen as the general manager a man

called Dr Fadlu-Dean. He was a Krio and a local businessman as well as a medical doctor. He also owned a fleet of buses. To me, he was the biggest rogue of all, as we found out later. On various sites, we had to employ people local to that area. One of the areas we were mining was rented by a member of parliament, who was expecting great things from the operation. I came to see that nobody could be trusted, as they would steal the teeth out of your mouth if you yawned!

I knew that it wouldn't be easy to get the trucks up to Lake Sonfon, as the country was very tropical and there were a lot of small rivers to cross. I found an old map showing a very small road going most of the way to the area. With the Volkswagen Kombi and a driver, I set off to see what it was like. I had to go and meet with the paramount chief of that area, explain what our role was and what we were going to do. He was quite happy with the situation and volunteered to come along with us, which would help ease the situations along the way, as we would be going through a lot of villages which would have their own chiefs. Also, it would give him the chance to meet and greet the people who were under his chiefdom, which he had not had the chance to do before. It was my job to map everything out. There were no actual roads, just paths, just wide enough for an ordinary car. I had to mark out how wide they would have to be for the equipment to get through. When we came to a river, it was made possible to cross by logs being thrown across, usually palm trees. The rivers were always at the bottom of a slope. I got to thinking that the best way to move the equipment through was to buy up a lot of surplus railway wagons, which were solid, well made and quite long. I could take the wheels off and use the bases as a bridge.

We had quite a long journey, and along the way we

collected village chiefs. We ended up with a Kombi full of chiefs. Then catastrophe happened. As usual, we got to a river crossing, and I got out at the top of the rise to take measurements and sketch the terrain. This particular time, as the Kombi drove down to the river, the driver picked the wrong line of logs. As the Kombi neared the other side, it started to slide off into the river, which was about six feet below. Luckily, the front bumper somehow got hooked on the pegs that held the logs together. The hilarious thing was to see all the chiefs jumping out of the doors and windows! It's a shame I didn't have a video camera, else I would have made £250 from You've Been Framed! So, what happens next? There were no phones and nobody to call for help. We were stuck in the middle of Africa. While I was pondering what to do, they must have sent somebody off into the bush, because, as I got down to the bottom, all of a sudden something magical happened. All these Africans came out of the bush, jumped into the water and virtually lifted the Kombi back onto the bridge. There were a lot of them. We then went on to the next village, from where they had obviously come, and celebrated. What an experience that was!

On arrival at one of the villages, the women and children ran off screaming as I climbed out of the Kombi. What was going on here? It seems that something they said in that village to keep children in line was, "You had better behave, or the white man will come and eat you!"

We worked seven days a week, beginning most days at 6am or 7am and working until late at night, between 9pm and 11pm. I had guys working nights trying to pump the holes out and drain the water so that we could get more gravel out. The diamond-bearing gravel was very deep, and digging down through sand and rocks to reach it was hard work. Gold and diamond gravel are different, but both are very heavy. You could look for diamonds in the gravel and then gold in the black sand. I paid a woman to pan it at a rate of two leones a day (a lot of money!).

On one of the sites we worked on, there was nowhere for me to sleep. I used to say, "Go ahead, sort yourselves out, and then find me somewhere to sleep at night." In this particular place, there was nothing, and all we could come up with was a lean-to on the side of somebody's hut, which had a corrugated iron roof, a single wood-framed window and a door. We were storing equipment in there. The bed I had to make up out of branches, managing to build up something so that I was off the floor, with cardboard on top as bedding. I do not recommend it for anybody. It would get so hot in there that I would have to sit outside until about 11pm each night before I could even think about going in, even then leaving the window and door open. I would sit out and read or strum my guitar by the light of an oil lamp or torch.

One evening, at about 7pm, I was sitting outside when Mr Soloman, a Lebanese gentleman, came past. He had a big store where we used to buy a lot of equipment, including meshes for when we were washing the diamonds. He had come to speak to me about some tools we had ordered, and he asked where I was staying. When I told him I was sleeping in the lean-to, he took one look and said, "Grab your things together and come with me. You're not staying here; you're staying in my compound." Believe you me, he had a massive compound. I had a proper bedroom where I could hang my mosquito net above me, a toilet, room for storing the equipment we weren't using on site at the time and a table and chairs. What a super guy to help me out like that. All he wanted in return was that if any of us went down to Freetown, we were to bring him a bottle of whisky. He didn't want any rent. This guy also made the best Turkish coffee you could ever imagine. Boy, it was strong! The spoon used to stand up in it, and it took some getting used to, but it was good.

When it came to washing, there were no toilets or anything on these sites, just huts. The children would carry me up a bucket of water on their heads, which was amazing in itself, because a bucket of water is a heavy thing. I have washed in some weird places. I tried a river once, but I just couldn't put up with it. It was cold and embarrassing to stand there where people could see you. In one of the villages, I asked if anyone had a toilet. In the middle of the village, they had this hut, and that was the toilet. You had to take a light in with you, and it was just a hole in the ground. When that hole was nearly full, they would just dig another one and put all the soil on top of the first one to fill it in. I used to take my bucket of water in there with me and have a wash at the same time. They were all very clean people and would religiously wash themselves, but the smell of that single toilet certainly wasn't the best. It was just one of those things I had to make the best of in that situation.

Another remarkable experience I had out there was when I had some money stolen. We had built a hut at the side of the river where we could store some of our equipment at night, leaving someone to sleep there guarding the site. This particular day of working on the ore washing machine (jig), I was getting very wet from the spray. I took the money I intended to use to buy food and fuel, about 80 leones, out of my shorts pocket and put it into the haversack in which

I kept my journal. The haversack was kept in the hut each day, and I would collect it from the hut at the end of the day before heading back to the compound to share the evening's food. Each morning, the Africans would come and pick me up from my digs to head down to the site in the Kombi. A few of the lads had stayed with me from working at Rutile and Sieromco and were very loyal to me.

This particular day, when I felt in my pocket for the money to pay for the day's meal, which usually came to about three and a half leones, I found that my pockets were empty. Then I remembered that I had put my money in my haversack. I looked through my bag but could find no money. There were about five boys with me, and when I explained what had happened, they had a whip-round to pay for the food. Two of them said, "Leave it to us," and then took the Kombi while the rest of us walked the mile or so down to the site through the villages. We had agreed not to say a thing about the missing money to the rest of the workers and just carry on as normal.

When the two boys arrived back, they explained what we had to do: for every one of the 30 or so men who had been on site the day before, we would collect the same amount of stones or pebbles and bury them in the ground. They then had another whip-round and gathered about 30p between them, which one of the lads then buried in the ground away from the site, near the trees by the river. Later on, in the afternoon, the same two lads took the Kombi, went off somewhere and brought back a witchdoctor. When the witchdoctor came, he looked nothing like what I had expected. He just looked like a normal African in his 20s or 30s, dressed in shorts and a shirt. He brought an interpreter with him, and he told us to draw two big lines in the sand about six feet apart with a circle in the middle and a line at one end. Then the witchdoctor took his shirt off and started rubbing oil on his body, which started shaking. Then he set off running all over the place. I wondered what he was doing and was told he was sniffing out the area. He came back to where we were, then set off running again, this time going to find the money that had been buried. The lads told me that if he found that money, he would be able to find the person who had taken my 80 leones. The 30 or so of us were assembled at the lines in the sand, 15 or so to each side. What happened next was really weird. The witchdoctor started going around sniffing everybody and dragging out various people into the line at the end. Then he took one to the circle. This went on for quite a while until he had about 9–10 guys separated out. The atmosphere was electric. God, if my mother could see me then, she would have gone mad! Everybody was terrified and thinking that the witchdoctor might pick them out next. Suddenly, the witchdoctor jumped on the man in the circle. If the rest of us hadn't stopped him and pulled him off, he would have killed this guy. He was like an animal. The guy he was attacking was quivering and saying, "I'm sorry, I'm sorry, it was me. I didn't mean it." Then, off the witchdoctor ran towards the village. I asked the interpreter where he was going, and he said, "He'll go and find what's left of your money." He ran straight into the village to the hut where this guy had buried the money he had stolen and brought it back to me – about 65 leones. I had to fire the lad, obviously, and he was a nervous wreck, but he survived. I then paid the witchdoctor and had enough money for us to carry on work for another week or so. I asked the lads what they called this witchdoctor, and they said that the name in English translates as 'the looking ground'. Obvious really, as he was looking in the ground. How do you explain that? What an experience!

Another strange happening took place whilst we were looking for diamonds in early 1981. We were trying to extract diamond bearing gravel from the middle of a river and were still using primitive methods, as our equipment still had not arrived. The rivers were very wide but not too deep, around chest or chin deep, as this was around the end of the dry season. We had a couple of small Briggs & Stratton pumps, which I managed to sit on floats. I put some hoses together to reach the bank. As we were trying to suck up the gravel in the river, we were just getting the sand and silt constantly falling into the hole we were making. I got hold of three 50gal. drums, cut the top and bottom off of each and then split them. I opened them out and made a circle with them, which I used to hold back the sand like a cofferdam. We could then push a six-foot pipe down into the water. As we sucked in the gravel, the pumps were pumping it off to shore so that we could store it.

I had a gang of about 15 working with me, and at any one time there were between five and seven of us in the water. After one group had been in the water for about an hour, they would swap over with another group. At one stage, after I had been in the water for quite a long time, I was walking out towards the shore when I heard this almighty scream. As I turned around, I saw a figure come out of the water and run past me, screaming his head off. When he reached the shore, he collapsed flat out. I shut the pump down and went over to him. It was Sammy Bangura, one of my lieutenants. I put him into the recovery position. Then the rest of the gang who were in the water also ran out yelling. They were all jabbering on about devils in the water.

I realised we weren't going to be able to carry on working, so I started to dismantle everything.

As I was bringing all of the equipment back to shore, all of a sudden, Sammy jumped up and raced back into the water where the hole was. About four of the lads ran after him, grabbed him and dragged him back to the shore. Then Sammy seemed to snap out of it and started saying, "I'm OK now. I'm fine." What all that was about, I have no idea to this day. We got all the equipment locked away, and I gave them all the day off. I asked the gang leader what we should do, and he said that we had to get a witchdoctor to provide a libation ceremony. I said, "Do what you've got to do," and off he went to sort it out. To me, this was scary. The next day, a witchdoctor came. As before, he was also dressed in ordinary clothes. We had to buy a goat, and he cut its throat, letting it bleed into the river – horrible! The ceremony took between half an hour and an hour, with us all standing around watching. He messed around with leaves and other bits and bobs, saying a lot of mumbo-jumbo. After the ceremony, we got to keep the goat, so at least that was food for quite a few days! They cut off the hooves and the head, chopped the rest up and it went in the pot. You name it, the tail, the lot. I managed to get them to give me bits without any fur on them!

After a couple of days, I sat down quietly with Sammy, away from the others, and asked him what the heck had happened in the water. Sammy and a couple of the other guys who had been with me for a while were from a different tribe to the other lads, who were local to where we were working. There is always a bit of conflict and disharmony in situations like that. My lads stuck together, and I stuck with them. They were all honest, good lads and very loyal to me. I mentioned earlier that when Ron had left Rutile and had gone to work for the ex-judge (the casino owner), I had given him a toolbox full of tools and that Sammy was the one who had taken them to Ron. Well, when Ron went back to the States and I was working at Sieromco, Sammy came back with that heavy toolbox on his shoulder. He had come over 150mi. to bring it back to me and had even sold his clothes to pay for bus fares. I reimbursed him and was amazed at his honesty. I found that most Africans weren't that honest with me, but Sammy always was. If he had said, "The toolbox was stolen, boss," I would have believed him. My lads, like Sammy, were very loyal to me because I looked after them. If Sammy or any of them had a relative who was ill or who had died, I would pay out of my pocket for them to go home to sort the situation out, understanding that they had their own lives to lead.

This day by the river, Sammy told me that, while he was in the water, something had grabbed him from below and pulled him down. When you were in the water, visibility was very bad; if you looked down into the water, it was just black, so he didn't know what it was. With all his strength, he had just thrown himself out of the river to get away from whatever it was. The only thing I could think of by way of an explanation was that somebody had perhaps been swimming past. Maybe the swimmer's legs had got tangled with Sammy's and Sammy had panicked? I don't know. It was the only idea I could come up with. I couldn't see it being anyone trying to play a joke, but I can't explain it for certain. I got Sammy back into the water quietly, saying, "Come on, get back in and swimming again." He did, and he was fine.

Others would mine in much deeper rivers that could be

10–12ft deep in the middle. The method used was to get two dug-out canoes and tie them together: one with the men and a little pump in it, the other empty. They go out to the middle of the river and get the pump going, then one guy jumps down into the water with a couple of rocks tied to his waist and the pipe from the pump in his mouth. He goes down there with a shovel, and they lower a bucket on a rope down to him. He starts putting sand in the bucket, and the other lads pull it up. They can be there all day, until the second canoe is full of collected sand. Whether they swap with the guy in the water, I don't know. How scary is that? Breathing compressed air for a long period isn't going to do anyone much good. In this simple method, the sand would be falling back into where the last shovelful came from, and they would be gathering rubbish. Our method was better because of the opened-out drums keeping the rest of the sand out. The diamond gravel is far below the surface layers and difficult to get to.

Washing the gravel was a very serious thing, and we had to be careful to make sure there wasn't any theft or cheating. This was quite an experience. We would have two or three experienced washers and then at least six more keeping an eye on what they were doing, because some of the tricks guys would try to pull were unbelievable. Luckily, I had Corporal Conteh, who was so straight you wouldn't believe. He had been in the army for years, then worked for Taylor Woodrow before coming to work for me as security. He and his younger brother would not let anything get past them.

Washing the ore is similar to panning for gold: continually swishing off the sand and gravel to separate the diamonds, as the diamond-bearing gravel is heavier than the gravel and sand. If and when a washer found a diamond, they would be paid depending on the size, one or two leones, just to keep them going and keep them on our side. After half an hour or so, when they had finished scooping off the sand and gravel and had removed any diamonds, they would turn the mesh over on a flat surface, empty it out and then go through what was left in there to find the industrial diamonds, which were brown or green. You could spot them quite easily, and there would normally be one in each mesh, or maybe two if you were lucky.

One of the tricks a washer could try was simple sleight of hand. When they were swishing the ore around and they spotted a diamond, they would wash it out of the mesh and into their hand, then drop it where they were standing and put their foot over it to press it into the earth. Then they would come back at night and dig it up. Another trick was shown to me by a guy I knew and used to help out from time to time. As he was swishing the ore, he said, "I want you to pick out a nice, coloured stone and keep your eye on it. Tell me when you don't see it any more." He shook the ore around and around and then, all of a sudden, the stone disappeared. I said, "Woah, it's not there." He stopped the swirling and then spat the stone out of his mouth! What he had done was work the stone to the side of the pan, put his hand under the edge of the pan and then hit it as he was bent over. With the impact of his hand, the stone had jumped straight up out of the pan and into his open mouth. How clever was that! The diamonds we were finding would be one or two carats, so probably a value of between £300 and £600 each, although this is only a rough estimate.

I would often be looking after two or three sites at a time. Ron, meanwhile, would spend more time at Lake Sonfon than I did. As I have said, Lake Sonfon was up in the north of Sierra Leone, in the mountains and really out in the wild. Food was always scarce in remote areas. Ron used to buy shotgun shells, which he would give to a hunter to go and get food for him. We could get rice, but meat was scarce. Every day, the hunter would come back with something, usually a monkey. Whenever I was up north, it would be monkey and rice for tea – not bad, but not the same as steak and chips!

On one of my early trips to Lake Sonfon, I left my site at about 8pm to head up to the lake. It was a long journey and would take all day, or in this case all night, to get there. After running out of road, we were driving on a bush track, and I was asleep in one of the seats near the back of the Volkswagen Kombi. It was very dark. Suddenly, I found myself on the floor. I got back up on the seat and tried to get back to sleep. Bang, I was on the floor again. I knew the roads were very rough, so I just accepted it. The next thing I knew, I was back down again.

I said, "What the heck's going on here?"

The driver said, "I'm trying to catch tomorrow's dinner."

Sure enough, he had this animal in his headlights and was trying to strike it. Eventually, he did, and it was thrown into the storage area. It was a large bush cat of some description. We lived on that for the next couple of days, with rice on the side!

You couldn't complain. The food always tasted OK, mainly because of the peppers that were always used to give it flavour. When we were working by rivers, people would sometimes come around with peeled oranges. I would get one for each of the lads and have about three or four myself. You couldn't chew them, but it was good to suck the juice out of them. Sometimes there would be bananas and peanuts too. I felt healthy enough on that diet. Everybody got diarrhoea now and again, but you get that anywhere in Africa!

Just prior to everything going wrong, Ron's wife, Paulette, flew out to Sierra Leone along with three guys. One of them was Robert Agar, who was a similar age to me. The two others were called Ray and Tom. I think the only mining experience the three of them had was maybe a little gold mining. Robert was living in his car in Cave Junction at the time. I only met Ray and Tom briefly, and then Ron took them to work up on Mr Kabba-Sei's area, the government minister. Ron left Ray and Tom with a vehicle and explained what they were to do to dig up the ore. I took Robert to another site and stayed with him until he knew what we were about. By this time, we had a large bungalow on the outskirts of Freetown with enough rooms to accommodate us all. Believe it or not, Ron had even had a larger bed made to fit his great height!

A short while later, when I went to check on how Robert was coping, he told me about a mistake he had made early on. One of the washers had found a diamond and had held it up for him to see. He had not recognised it as a diamond and had thought they were taking the mickey, so he had thrown it back in the river! They had all jumped in and started scraping about trying to find it. He was in the bad books for a while after that. The diamonds that we were finding looked a lot like small bits of rock and broken windshield, the difference being that the diamond has a silky sheen on it.

Unfortunately, our whole operation went – pardon the phrase – tits up. All the signs were good. We had a geologist who had planned out where we were going to mine. We had this ship full of equipment coming. We were going to have all the equipment we could possibly want: big diggers, D8s, you name it.

I mentioned earlier that when I had met Mr Spooner in Sierra Leone before we started work, he had told me that he'd had a full medical and been given 100%. He was later found dead of a heart attack. Then, we discovered there was $1 million missing from the company's African bank account. We had been drawing money out to live on and there was no money there! Mr Bentley froze all our assets and left us with nothing: no money whatsoever. We were unaware of the situation with Mr Spooner and the missing $1 million at this stage, but this was the start of the downfall of the whole thing. I had sorted out storage for the equipment that was to arrive, and Ron and I went to Freetown to meet the ship. The captain of the ship met up with us, and we took him for a nice meal. He was a great guy, but when he got back to the ship, he got a message from Bentley saying, "Turn the ship around and bring it back to Galveston." We knew nothing about this at the time and only found out about it much later. It took a while for Ron and me to become aware of what was happening, because communication was so limited. There were no telephones. Communication was by telex machine. I think in the whole country they had one outside line, and you could never get on that. It was only when I worked for companies like Sierra Rutile that they might have their own communications systems. We had two-way walkie-talkies which were meant to be arriving on the boat so that we could speak to each other at distance.

Days later, Ron got a message from this Dr Fadlu-Dean saying that he had to fly to London with him to meet Bentley and Brissette. We asked why and were told that the company was 'having problems'; that was all we knew. Ron collected about 15 diamonds and some gold to smuggle out with him to show Bentley the quality of what we were finding. Don't forget, we were mining in such a primitive way at this stage. I don't know what this guy expected. One area they told us to mine had been mined out six times before, but we still found the odd diamond there. The vehicle we used most at that stage was a Toyota twin cab. It was very basic and primitive inside – just tin. When we were transporting diamonds and gold for Ron to take to London, I would put them in a bag, remove a panel in the cab of the Toyota and drop the bag inside so that it was out of sight. The only people who knew we were transporting diamonds and gold at this particular time were Ron, Fadlu-Dean and me. Whether he told some of his men or not I don't know. This is where the story gets intriguing.

Ron wasn't taking a suitcase with him, just an overnight bag, since he was only going over to London for the weekend or so. Back then, you could bribe your way through into the departure lounge, which I did. I was sitting in there waiting for Ron to come through, having had his bag checked in and come through passport control. Fadlu-Dean came through quickly, but Ron was delayed. When he finally got through, he was all flustered. He explained that he had been taken away and strip searched. Luckily, I was the one carrying the diamonds and was planning to pass them to Ron just as he was getting on the plane. I was beginning to get worried, as it seemed as if there was a plot against us. The officials obviously knew what they were looking for with Ron. I took him to one side, away from Fadlu-Dean, and explained about the customs system in England. This was in the early 1980s, and, from what I could remember, there would be two lines: a 'nothing to declare' and a 'something to declare'. I told Ron that he could go through the nothing to declare line, and, as far as I knew, they would only select one in ten people to search. If selected, they would find the diamonds on him, which hadn't been weighed and registered as they legally should have been, and he would end up in jail on a serious charge.

I said, "This is your choice. What do you want to do?"

As they were about to board, he turned to me and said, "You keep them, Pete."

As he was getting on the plane, two more people ran across, grabbed Ron and took him away. He was gone another half hour or more before they finally let him back on the plane. Putting two and two together, this to me seemed like Fadlu-Dean was behind it, as it was only the three of us who knew about the plan to take diamonds out of the country.

I went back to Freetown, and Paulette was there. I decided not to tell her what had happened. Suddenly, Ray and Tom, who had been up at Kabba-Sei's plot, burst in through the door. These guys were in a real state. They had been virtually kicked off the site by an irate member of parliament who had accused them, us and the company of all sorts. He had said that he was going to sue us. He knew that the ship with all the equipment had turned back, which was something that at this stage neither Ron nor I even knew! He was going to lose face with all his peers, to whom he had obviously been bragging about how rich he was going to be by working with this big American mining company. Ray and Tom had just packed up the gear and driven back to Freetown to find out what the hell was going on. You can't blame them. This was the first time I had heard anything about the ship going back.

Seeing that everyone was upset, I suggested that we have a night out at the Cape Sierra Hotel. I thought we could meet up with some old friends there who I thought would cheer them up. These old friends were a white father-and-son team who were mining for diamonds with a decent set-up that they owned and their head of security, Big John Smith. The father and son were really funny, like a double act, and had some super stories. They also owned a go-kart track somewhere on the east coast of the States. John was about six feet two and had been a bodyguard for various people. I used to meet John up country on my trips; I would take some food and a couple of beers and stay for a while. After I had known him for a long time, I started to think he had been a hitman too, but what a nice guy he was. He was from Arizona and was super friendly. One of the people for whom he had worked was Evel Knievel, when he tried to jump the Snake River and failed miserably. There was a riot thereafter, and John was in the middle of it, battling with everybody. He had scars all over his hands, arms, face and body.

Whilst Paulette, Ray, Tom and I were driving to the hotel, which was over 20mi. away, I noticed that we were being followed. When we arrived, we sat in the lounge, and I noticed that we were being watched. I still had the diamonds and gold in the truck at this point. When Big John finally arrived, he looked really distressed. He called me over and said, "Please buy me a drink; I have no money." I bought a couple of drinks, and we all sat down. John then began to tell us his story. He had just got down from up country that afternoon, and the father for whom he worked had collared him and said, "We need you to take us to the ferry quickly, now!" The ferry was over an hour's drive from Cape

Sierra. The father, son and John all jumped in the Jeep, and the father drove. All they told John was that tickets had just arrived for them and that the two of them had to catch a flight. John asked why one of the drivers that were on the payroll wasn't going with them. They said that every driver had some sort of reason why they couldn't go. I was sitting there listening to this story, thinking there was a conspiracy going on here against all of us. When they had got to the ferry, they were running late and panicking. The barrier was coming down, and the Jeep hit it. It didn't break the barrier, but it knocked it flying upwards. They went straight to the jetty where the ferry was leaving, jumped out of the Jeep, grabbed their bags from the back and threw them onto the ferry. Then the father and son had to take a running jump to make it onto the ferry itself, and they waved John goodbye. Security then ran down and surrounded John and the Jeep. They sent for the special police, who searched John and stripped the Jeep out all over the floor. They had him there for over an hour. John tipped out all the money he had in his pockets and said, "Look, guys, this is all I have. I've got to go." They took the money and let him go. He had just arrived back when he met us at the hotel.

While John was telling us his story, I was looking around all the time and spotting all these undercover policemen dotted about the lounge. There weren't that many people in the lounge at the time. There were two at a table near to us with no drinks, who kept moving to other tables and were obviously trying to listen to what we were saying. Finally, at closing time, we had to leave. As we walked out to the cars, we were followed out. They jumped into cars parked just further up the road to ours. Knowing that we had been followed and watched all night, I thought it was likely that on the way home we would be pulled over and searched. When they found unregistered, illegal diamonds and gold in the truck, we would all be thrown in jail.

Time for Plan B! As we got to our vehicle, I said to Paulette, Ray and Tom, "Don't ask why, but look under the bonnet, will you? Reckon to be doing something there while I have a chat with John." I then asked John, "Have you anywhere safe that I could hide these diamonds, and I'll pick them up in a day or so when it's safe?"

He replied, "Yeah, no problem. I've got places."

I undid the panel, pulled out the bag and passed it to John. We were followed as we started driving home, but then I managed to lose them in the backstreets of Freetown and got back to the house safe. A couple of days later, I ventured into Freetown and called in at the bar where all the ex-pats used to meet up and where we could get cheap meals for $2. There I met Mickey, a guy we all knew, who bought diamonds and took them back to Arizona, where he and his work partner would cut them and sell them. Mickey was a diamond dealer who had been on the African coast for years. His first words to me were, "Did you hear about John?" When I said no, he told me that John had been arrested late the other night. They had come around at about 3am and searched his room, where they had found the diamonds I had given him and a revolver. Even being in possession of a revolver in Sierra Leone was a serious thing, as a permit to have one had to be signed by the president himself. John was in deep shit, believe you me. John had hidden the diamonds in a panel in his bathroom behind the tiles. Whoever had cleaned his room must have found this panel and told the police about it. There was nothing I could do, but I felt terrible.

I used to drive up to the cape every day and ask whether anyone had heard anything about him. After about a week, John turned up. He was under house arrest and told not to leave the place. They had an armed officer with him to watch him. He told me that the hotel wouldn't feed him, but he was allowed to sleep there. I asked the guard if he minded if I took John to get some breakfast at a bar by the beach. The guard let us go but followed us down there. I did this for a week, going every day to make sure John was fed and had some money to buy beers and so on. I got him into the habit of telling the guard he was going for a swim every day. By that time, the guard would stay in the Cape Sierra, waiting for John. John would walk down the beach wearing jeans, a T-shirt, flip-flops and a towel draped over his haversack. John's plan was that, when he could, he would make it to his Jeep and drive to Monrovia, the capital of Liberia, in order to escape.

I said, "John, when the guard notices you're missing, they'll have guards looking for you."

However, the police didn't have John's passport, which had been hidden somewhere else when they had searched his room. Believe it or not, his name wasn't even John Smith; it was Norman something, and the photo only vaguely looked like him! In the meantime, during these days, I had been leaving my truck at John's hotel and driving his Jeep about for a couple of hours. I thought it would keep the police confused that often John's vehicle was gone, but he was still there. I then had to go up country for a couple of weeks, and I knew I couldn't leave him like that. I gave John the last $100 I had been saving and told him I would try to get hold of Mickey the diamond dealer and get him to telex their backer to send him a plane ticket out. When I got back from up country, John was gone. Nobody knew how he had got away, but I ended up with his Jeep, which we hid and then used up country. It wasn't until I met up with John in Phoenix much later that I found out how he had got away.

When Ron came back from England, it was time to get everyone up to speed. That night, we all – Ron, Robert, Tom, Ray, Paulette and me – sat down to decide what to do. Ron told me that the company had gone bust and that we were all fired. We in turn explained to Ron what had happened after the airport and that later that night we had been followed to the Cape Sierra. We told him that, whilst speaking to John, we had been observed by plain clothes police and that I had passed the diamonds to John in order to avoid being stopped and found in possession of them on our way back home. We explained that John was later arrested for being in possession of unregistered diamonds and gold, as well as a revolver.

I was left with no ticket home, and I'd had no wages for months, so I had no means with which to buy one. The potential for a successful operation was there, but they had left us to mine with primitive methods for months, and then the whole thing had collapsed. It just beggared belief. I was owed about $11,600 in all. Ray and Tom decided to catch the next flight home with Paulette, while Robert decided to stay on and try to sort out the sites with me and Ron.

The daily journal that I kept over the next few weeks gives a detailed log of how we had tried to sort out the sites during this time after the company failed, and it makes horrendous reading now. All the machines and the Land Rover were breaking down all the time, and we had no money to buy parts. We would get parts by giving our personal belongings, like my camera, as payment. We had no money for food and had to beg for bags of rice and borrow petrol. We sent the vehicles out as taxis to make some money to buy food. Sometimes Ron and I would have to go to the casino in Freetown, where Ron would borrow $100 to get started gambling. When we had won $600–700, I would leave to go back up country, where I could pay for the men's wages, petrol, rice and the spare parts for which we had begged, and we could carry on working for a couple of weeks. It was a joke. Ron spent most of this time in Freetown trying to get some sense out of the bank and Fadlu-Dean and raise some money. Meanwhile, Mr Brissette was still with us and on our side. He was trying to find backers to buy out the company from Bentley. Below is an extract from the journal I kept:

Saturday, 16th May 1981, Masanbendu

Both machines (pumps) were broken. Went to Jawena and bought a water seal. No money left so had to leave my camera and a zoom lens to cover the cost. We got one pump to work, repaired the other and managed to get a room to sleep in. Moses the mechanic spoilt the seal and I had to go back to the store. I borrowed 30 leones as a deposit to get two new seals which cost 60 leones each, leaving me owing them 90 leones. Kabba-Sei's brother stopped us from washing. The washing jig was damaged by an experienced Caterpillar driver whilst lifting the jig off the pick-up, so I had to repair that. I had to send for a mechanic to fix one of the other machines and pay him 10 leones, but I could only give him 7. I finished repairing the jig by 11pm. Rain is heavy. One pump left to keep the water down.

Sunday, 17th May 1981
Rained all night and morning. Arranged a ceremony. One pump seized up. Took out the water seal and put it in another pump. Fixed the seized pump, pulled gravel by 5.30pm. Moved it to the bank and struggled to keep the water down. Couldn't take the jig for two reasons – no petrol and no pump until the man gets back from Freetown with seals.

Monday, 18th May 1981
Ran out of oil. Went to Jaima for oil and points at a cost of 20 leones, cannot afford. No petrol, sent the vehicle as a taxi. Still cannot get to the other site with the washing jig. Only one pump still working. Removed two piles of gravel into one big one. Sent David Tommy (an African hired by Fadlu-Dean as a site boss) to borrow petrol, 26 gallons, 6 for the Toyota and 20 for the pumps and the rest of the site.

Tuesday, 19th May 1981
Transported jig to Bamba Kunya. Problems starting the diesel engine on the jig, also the pump. Left at 3.30pm. Pete Whondo reported that the Land Rover was in a ditch a long way off. A track road had parted, and they were lucky to be alive. Gathered ropes and men to pull it out. Sorted it out and got it back on the road. Gear trouble, breakdown again. Ron met us repairing it at 6pm. Later, Ron stripped the Robin pump and got it working. We finished at 10pm.

Wednesday, 20th May 1981
Ron and I went to Bamba Kunya to check on the jig. Met Kabba-Sei's brother, Brima. Jig working except hand starting of the diesel engine. Ron took the Toyota and left me with the jeep (John's). Ron arranged for us to borrow another 40 gallons – 5 gallons for each vehicle and 30 gallons for the site. We arranged for BK Mussa to start the pumps at 5am.

Thursday, 21st May 1981
Was on the site by 6am. Neither machine working. Robin couldn't start, the brig's blocked. Sent for Whondo (the mechanic). He should have been there at 5am. As we tried to sort things, the bank collapsed, swamping everything. A letter came from Kabba-Sei. He wanted us to set the jig up to wash on Sunday. I had to say no chance, Ron took the Toyota (which we use for transporting the jig) and I have no means of hiring any other vehicle. Repaired two broken starters for the brigs. Whondo broke the rope on the starter on the Robin. At 12 noon I went to borrow a machine from another site at Bamba Kunya. They were stopped, lack of water. I had to dig a channel to bring the water back to the pumps. They hadn't thought to do that. On returning, pump not working, wire broke inside also at points, condenser took from another one. Took off the manifold from the Land Rover to weld up the leaks, no avail. As problems mounted up, must sell the Land Rover. Cecil Brissette okayed it as it cost too much to run with constant repairing. Got one pump running, ran all night to have the pit empty for morning.

Friday, 22nd May 1981
Started at 6.30am. Pit was empty enough. 9am went to Sefadu to try to sell the Land Rover. The man said no way after one look, he didn't want to know and wouldn't buy it. Got back, rice finished. Borrowed one bag. The robin's not working. We were just eating rice and any leaves and peppers we could find.

Saturday, 23rd May 1981
Had to borrow money to go to Freetown. Left instructions with Whondo to help Brad with his Volkswagen engine dredge and then service all our machines. David Tommy to use the Land Rover to earn money for food. Had to borrow petrol to get to Freetown. Ron and I went back to the casino. Borrowed $100 so we had enough to pay our debts and carry on.

Wednesday, 27th May 1981
Drove all night. Arrived back at Masanbendu at 11.30am. Whondo was missing, no machines serviced, Land Rover not running, starter problem. Went to Bamba Kunya for the jig. Arrived at 2pm. Everybody had finished, had to round them up to load the jig. Took quite a few of us to lift it into the Toyota's back. Then went to collect our equipment from where it was stored. Was told that until we had paid 30 leones rent for storing our equipment they wouldn't let us have it. They were charging 3 leones a day for 10 days that we were on the site. After arguing I got away with paying them 6 leones. Got back at 5pm, no sign of Kabba-Sei and found Pete Whondo back. Asked David Tommy for a full report of what he did. Got a report that two drums of diesel were missing. David Tommy said he gave them to Brad, and until Brad gets back from

Freetown I won't know what happened.

Thursday, 28th May 1981
No sign of Kabba-Sei or his brother. Heavy rain from 7.30am to 9am. Machines set. Pumps set. Trench for sluice box all ready. Can't start until Kabba-Sei arrives. Only one pump working, so can't really drain. Went to Sefadu to find out about Kabba-Sei. Found his brother, who said he would come early tomorrow.

Friday, 29th May 1981
Still waiting for Kabba-Sei's brother. One day's rice left. Sent the Land Rover out as a taxi. Just enough money for one bag of rice and some sauce. The brother arrived about 9.45am and we started. Still waiting for Brad to borrow a gold saver off him. Had started to make one back in Freetown but ran out of funds to continue. We washed the gravel at 11.45am, then again at 2.15pm, then again at 4.15pm. Nothing was found. We washed black sand for gold and found not even a pennyweight. Land Rover made 4 leones and used up all the petrol – not good at all. Washed again at the end of the day – nothing, no diamonds or gold. Sent the Toyota out as a taxi, came back with 2 gallons of petrol and 5 leones – not good. It rained from 8pm onwards. Things starting to get desperate. Little money to feed us and get petrol for machines.

Saturday, 30th May 1981
Sent the Toyota out as a taxi at 7am for money for petrol. Machines working fine. We've got to find something. Toyota back at 11.30am with 20 leones and 4 gallons of petrol. No diamonds yet. Just a few hours of work left for

tomorrow. Things are desperate.

Sunday, 31st May 1981
Raining very heavy. Late start. Sent the Toyota out as a taxi at 7am. If Ron doesn't appear, I'll go to Yengama to get plugs and points for the Land Rover to keep it running. Could only get plugs, no points. Said my farewells to Phil and Linda as this would be the last time I would see them. They have been really good friends to me. Finished running the gravel through the jig after pulling petrol out of all the other machines to keep the pump running. Washed 100 tonnes of gravel.

Monday, 1st June 1981
The workers were worried about money and food. Spoke to them and told them Ron was trying to get money for them. Siphoned petrol out of the Toyota for the Land Rover to use as a taxi. I had enough to get to Makali, where I borrowed enough petrol from Issa to get me to Freetown.

That trip to Freetown on 1st June was the end of our mining in Sierra Leone. We couldn't do any more – and I never got my camera back!

There was always the odd Peace Corps worker from America that we would come across during out time in Sierra Leone. The organisation sent them out to Africa to work on various silly schemes. In our area, near to where we were mining, we had met this young American lad. He had nothing; I just couldn't believe it. As I was packing up to leave, I decided that I would give him all my stuff, including my mosquito net and my water filter. You had to boil water twice before you even put it in the filter and then boil it again after it came out of the filter, before you made tea or coffee with it. When water was brought to me, it came from the same place in which everyone washed, and animals and people would both wee there; it wasn't like water at home, and of course you couldn't buy bottled water back then either. I gave him a torch, a kettle and whatever else I had. You name it, I passed it on to him, because I didn't need it any more. I felt sorry for him. The Peace Corps would send them out to these backward countries, and they didn't understand the situation in which these guys were living. This guy could have come down with all sorts of diseases.

Now stuck in Freetown with no way of getting home, Ron put together a telex for me to send to Bentley as follows:

> I have read your comments to Dr Dean concerning my termination and I could hardly believe it. How could you, or your associates, hire someone like myself, go for a period of four months before reimbursing my airfare and then short me £5, not including the interest I had to pay. No salary was paid to me until the fifth month, and that was only $2,000, which is $600 short of one month's pay. You tried to leave me in a foreign country, where expenses are two and a half times those of my home country, without money or return airfares and still owing me in excess of $11,600. My embassy and also the US embassy here in Freetown have been consulted and have advised me to send you this telex as a personal request to resolve our business before they get involved. I have sent a handwritten letter, via Mrs Finger, requesting that you release the balance of my salary to her in cash or via a cheque that she can deposit in her account so that Mr Finger can then give me a personal cheque. When

can I expect to be paid and receive a ticket for my return home?

Awaiting your reply,

Pete North (24th May 1981)

This one is from Ron to Bentley:

Mr Bentley,

I have tried my best for you and your company, but you seem not to care too much. You have ruined my name and reputation both back home and here by not meeting your obligations to the people I was asked to arrange credit with for your company. The current creditors of the company have lost all confidence in us. The gravel that Pete and I have worked day and night to extract from the two remaining mines cannot be washed until the salaries and other debts that were made so that the employees and ourselves could eat are paid.

Dr Fadlu-Dean has 14 pieces which came from a small amount of gravel compared with what we now have at Konta. We have several tonnes of gravel at Massabindu, which has also never been washed. Baama or Isatu's property was closed after washing there. We recovered 54 pieces, which she [Isatu, who owned one of the sites] will not release until she is paid. There is no way to divide a parcel in half fairly.

You have removed Pete and I from the payroll, and that means everything will be lost. When we leave, and we must leave because there is no food and no money, the thieves will come in short order and take all the equipment. I've asked the doctor to sell the diamonds he has, but he refused. You have directed all correspondence to him in the past, but if you ever reply to me, send it to me personally.

Also, your relatives have made things very uncomfortable for my family in Cave Junction by telling everyone in town that we do not do business with you, that I have been fired and the company closed down. I'd also like to know if and when you're going to do something for Pete North. It only causes me further embarrassment and disgrace, because I have asked him to trust Jim [Bentley's son] and Carl [Jim's accountant], and they assured him that he would be paid. My father has a serious operation in Boise, and I will be leaving here soon, but I hope you will reply before I am to leave. I have sold my personal belongings and paid back most of the cash I have borrowed, which means that I have spent 7,460 leones to keep things together and also keep it safe for me to travel.

By the way, no one has cancelled the power of attorney that Jim made out to me. I checked yesterday, and Paulette has returned to the US with the receipts that you requested and has passed them on to Cecil Brissette.

Back to me, and I received a telegram from Bentley which said the following:

At the meeting with Ron Finger, Cecil Brissette and Fadlu-Dean on 14th April in London, it was concluded that, with reduced activity in Sierra Leone, your employment would not be required after 30th April 1981 and that I would not provide you with funds to pay you under any agreement

you might have with BB&S after that date. Finger and
Dean were directed to inform you of the decision and
fully understood that if they continued your employment
after that date, they would have to supply the funds
from their own profit realised in Sierra Leone from their
own resources. I suggest that you buy your return ticket
using funds from your English account. We will pay
you whatever is remaining of our obligation under the
agreement that was terminated on 30th April into that
same account.

They hadn't paid me any money in ages, so was I going to believe them when they said that if I paid for my ticket, they would reimburse me? Of course not!

Finally, my ticket came through; Bentley must have paid for it. It arrived at the main travel company in Freetown, who informed me that it was there. This was on a Friday. The first plane out was on Saturday. I then set about putting my affairs in order. I had to borrow a large sum of money to pay off my debts: the petrol, the food and so on. I got the money from a Lebanese gentleman with whom we were friendly in Freetown. He was a nice guy. To lend me something like £500 was no small thing. I gave him my guitar, plus one I had been given by one of the Americans (Ray, who had left when the trouble had started), as security. The next day, Ron and I got Robert to take me to the plane (more on his story later).

Whilst all these problems with BB&S had been going on, I had been approached by Sieromco again to build some hoppers, equipment and buildings on their site back up country where I used to work. This meant that I would have another project to work on and that I could find work for the guys who had followed me through thick and thin, so

I intended to take it after my visit home.

When I returned to England, I then received a horrible phone call from Fadlu-Dean. He accused Ron, me and one other man (Robert) of stealing diamonds and gold from Lake Sonfon and Kabba-Sei's area (the member of parliament). It really blew me away and angered me so much. I wondered what he was on about. These accusations could only have come from Fadlu-Dean himself. He had also appointed one of his lieutenants, JS Kamara, to collect as much of the equipment and our personal effects as possible. I guess we were made scapegoats, and I didn't realise the severity of the situation until I received a telegram from a Mr Whoehrer, the general manager of Sieromco. It said that he had received a very disturbing letter about me and two others (Ron and Robert). It seems the letter came from BB&S, which meant Fadlu-Dean had spread the poison.

At the same time, I suffered another bout of malaria, which set me back a week before I could write to Fadlu-Dean and ask him what the hell he was doing. I sent him a five-page letter. I was a bit upset to say the least. As I have said, I was keeping a journal and writing reports the whole time, and I was able to piece them together, photocopy the pages and send them to him to explain what I had been doing and to make clear that I hadn't been stealing anything. My journal even included comments around the edges where I had written down explanations of why we had done certain things, as I knew that anyone who had no experience of site work wouldn't otherwise understand. I hadn't even been involved in the washing and finding of diamonds; I had stayed back during that part of the operation, so I couldn't be accused of anything. He never replied to my letter, and I never got a cent from them towards the $11,600 of wages

I was owed.

I would later find out that, during the collapse of the company, Mr Brissette had managed to get five backers lined up and ready to take over so that we could have carried on. One of the backers was the Jackson Five. In 1981, they had a lot of money, and Jermaine Jackson wanted to pay $5 million to Bentley and give us $1 million up front just to continue the operation. Bentley didn't want to know. We think that for some reason he wanted to write off the $5 million it had cost him to set up the company as a tax loss. Otherwise, why would he not accept that offer? As for the supposed missing $1 million that was meant to be in the bank for us in Sierra Leone, the only conclusion we could come to was that Mr Spooner was moving the money around and making money off it himself. That's only our opinion. When Spooner died, Bentley froze all his assets, leaving Spooner's wife destitute. Another conclusion we came to was that maybe Bentley had Spooner bumped off. You have to stack up the facts and ask yourself why. I know heart attacks can happen any time, but still …

As a footnote to the saga in Sierra Leone, it wasn't until I started writing this story, going through the various telexes and letters and thinking about everything that happened, that I realised that Fadlu-Dean never thought to ask Ron or me what happened to those diamonds that Ron was going to take to London for Bentley. Now, this is the crux of the matter really. I can't understand why Fadlu-Dean didn't question either Ron or me as to the whereabouts of those diamonds and gold. He was solely in charge, answering only to Bentley. If it had been me, it would have been my first question to either of us. I did see Fadlu-Dean every time I came down to Freetown, as I had reports typed out and handed in to him, so he had plenty of chances to ask me. The one exception was my last visit, the day when my ticket finally came through for my flight home the next day. Don't forget, when Robert got back from dropping Ron and me off at the airport, the police were at our house to arrest us. I believe to have us arrested could only have come from Fadlu-Dean. If I had told him that I was catching the Saturday flight and not the one that was scheduled for Monday, I am sure that the police would have come for us earlier. Then this story would never have been told, as I don't think that we would have got out alive. We were just someone to point the finger at and take all the blame. Believe you me, Robert had a bad time, as you will read in the next chapter. In the Freetown jails, they have a special room where they torture people. There was no way Robert wanted to go in there, and during his time in jail, he said, "You just tell me whatever you want me to say and I'll sign off on it." The president of the country at that time, Siaka Stevens, was the worst out of everybody; it is said that he had his own death squad and had people killed for fun. I believe he controlled all the diamonds through the National Diamond Company. One of the key operatives had been arrested years before for holding illicit diamonds.

Ron was in Freetown most of the time, fighting to save the company, while I was up country. It wasn't until I finally arrived in Cave Junction, Oregon, and had telephone conversations with Mr Brissette that I found out from him how the police had tried to turn the plane I was on back to Freetown. Fortunately for me, the plane was too far out of territorial waters. Also, Mr Brissette told me that Interpol had been informed to arrest Ron and me, but again, luckily for us, they ignored it. All this could only have come from Fadlu-

Dean's greed, as he collected all our equipment, the vehicles, my two guitars etc. I also found out that, after his own escape, Big John Smith had realised the trouble we were in and had tried to raise a band of mercenaries to get us out. Alas, he didn't have enough money to pull it off, but at least he was trying for us. At the time, I never even thought about talking to Fadlu-Dean about those diamonds; I was wrapped up in trying to save the operation of the company. I only really saw the immense danger we were in with hindsight.

Ron, Paulette and me at one of the sites

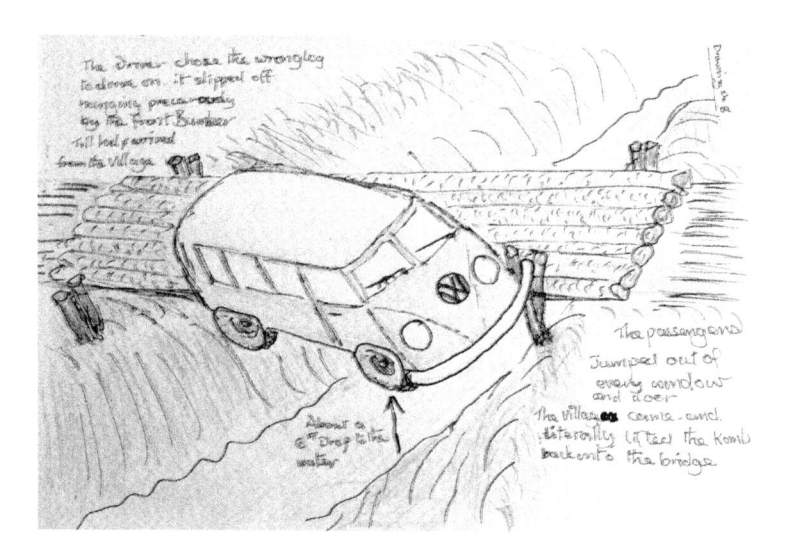

The Kombi that came off the bridge

The washing jig that I made

One of the sites we worked on showing the stacked ore, the hut, the jeep, the Kombi and the washing jig

Two guys are washing the ore and looking for diamonds. The rest are watching them, keeping an eye out for the tricks they can get up to, 1981

CHAPTER NINE
America

While I was recovering from the relapse of my malaria in England, I was in touch with Ron, who said that I should come out to the States where we could try to get some of my money from Bentley. I still had some savings, so I flew out there, and we tried to take Bentley to court. Nobody would take the case on. One guy we found said that he would pursue the case, but he wanted money up front. We couldn't find anyone to take it on a contingency. We were up against a multimillionaire; how were we going to win?

I settled down at Ron's house in Cave Junction. He also had a place of 240 acres up in the Redwood forests called Gilligan's Butte, which was beautiful. We used to go up to this place, which looked like something from The Beverly Hillbillies, and take a load of sausages and a crate of beer with us. We would make a barbecue, chop logs and have a great day. Ron had borrowed some mules, which were unbelievable. They only knew two words: one which meant 'stop', and the other meant 'go'. I could never remember them, which was a problem, because without the stop word they just kept going no matter what! It was summer, and every night we would sit out and end up singing songs. It never rained. As you drove through Oregon on the highway, you would see massive signs at the side of the road with a big arrow warning of the danger of forest fires. There were always people dropping in at the house all the time, and we had a good time for the few months that I stayed with them.

Most people who lived around the Cave Junction area were either hippies or logger-types. They all had long hair, big beards and wore checked shirts and jeans – real rednecks. One day, I went out to a place called O'Brien. It had one store and one bar, with a few houses scattered around. We were in this bar having a beer, and there were only three other people there plus the barman. After a while, a young lady came in wearing a kaftan and other hippy clobber.

She said, "Who's first?" and one of the three guys walked over and said, "I'm first."

What the hell was this? He got down on the floor, and she started to manipulate his back with chiropractic techniques. She went through all of them, including the barman, collected her money and then left. Where else would you see that?

It seemed that most of the hippies lived in the forest, sometimes in houses made out of cardboard boxes. Most of them grew pot. The summer there is a proper summer, dry and hot, so they didn't need lights and greenhouses like you would in the UK. They grew pot outside. Come autumn, they would harvest it and all drive down to California, where they would sell it and spend the winter. Then they would come back to Oregon in the spring. That was how they lived – just weird! I was led to believe shortly before I arrived there that somebody had shot down a police helicopter that had been buzzing the area.

I mentioned earlier that Robert Agar had driven me to the airport when I was leaving Sierra Leone. Well, around this time, while he was walking around town, Robert had his passport stolen. He then couldn't leave Sierra Leone until either he got a new one or he got some document from the American embassy. When Ron and I were leaving the country, we had given him all the money we had, both leones and dollars. When Robert arrived back at the house from the airport, the police were there. They had come to arrest Ron and me, as well as Robert. Robert was taken for an interview and was then thrown into a cell roughly 12ft square along with up to 50 Africans. No food was given, there was no toilet and nowhere to sleep. The cell was hosed down every day. They hadn't charged him, as he was just a pawn to them. He was fairly newly arrived, whereas Ron and I were the main people they were after. They let Robert keep the money we had given him, so every day he would buy a big dish of rice and sauce and feed everybody in the cell. In return, they really looked after him. They made a space for him to lie down at night. This went on for three or four weeks. Of course, we didn't know where he was. I was in England and Ron was in the States with no knowledge of any of it.

When Robert was down to his last couple of dollars, he managed to write a note telling the embassy where he was. He gave the last of his money to a person who was being released that day as payment for taking the note to the embassy. The embassy finally freed him and then stuck him in a flea pit until they sorted him a passport and gave him a ticket to New York. As he had no money, he set off to hitchhike back to Oregon, which was just short of 3,000mi.

While Robert had been up country in Sierra Leone, he had met up with the father and son I mentioned earlier, who were superb guys. They had told Robert what town they lived in back in the US and talked about the go-kart track they owned there. Somehow, Robert remembered the name of the town and managed to make his way there. They took pity on him and tried to fatten him up, as he had lost a lot of weight. They gave him an old car, filled it with petrol and gave him $100 to help him on his way. When his money ran out, Robert had to stop and find work in order to buy more food and petrol to keep moving on. It reminds me of the song, Me and You and a Dog Named Boo.

By the time Robert was working his way across the country like this, I was back in the States with Ron, and we were talking on the phone to Brissette a lot. He told us of Robert's arrest and how he had now been flown back to the US. It had been a while since he had left Africa, and we were worried for him, because we didn't know where he was. We didn't realise he'd only been flown to New York and not further west and were left wondering why he hadn't shown up.

While I was in Cave Junction, I would go to check out the two or three bars there and ask if anyone knew him or had seen him.

People seemed to be getting wary of the questions I was asking. It was then that I realised they thought I was an undercover police spy! I managed to sneak out through the back door of one place when I realised that I had overstayed my welcome. When Robert finally did show up, boy were we relieved. It was then that he told us his story of how he had crossed America.

Ron was a popular guy: everybody knew him, and there

were always people coming to the house. One day, he had some visitors, a lad of about 30 with four girls in tow. He was very good looking and there was a certain something about him that just made you sit up and take notice. He had charisma in spades and just lit up the room. The girls were his followers, groupies or whatever you want to call them, but in a nice way. They obviously liked his company so much. He was full of chat and was a really superb guy. When he left, it was like someone had turned the lights off. He obviously knew Ron and Paulette well and called at the house again on a few other occasions. One day, he came over and I found out that he had been involved in an accident at a wood yard in which he was working (to make money for Christmas). When working on a large planer, the timber had snagged on a knot and had taken his fingers in. He lost every finger on both hands, plus his thumbs. He was still the same person with the charisma and the girls, and he didn't let it get him down.

After he left, Ron noticed a tear on my cheek. Ron thought it was through seeing the injuries, but I was feeling for the lad and thinking about what his life would be like in the future, having to rely on someone else to fasten his buttons, tie his laces and so on. What sort of life would he have with just stumps to hold with? It was very sad. Seeing it tore me up. Later on, everyone in the valley went to finish a timber house that he had started to build. There were hundreds of us there, and everyone brought food, beer and tools. We all had a great time finishing his building in time for winter. It was a great experience. Alas, I never saw the lad again, as we went off trucking and never came back. I certainly tried to be a better person after meeting him, and I still wonder how he has survived after all these years.

While I was staying with Ron, we often used to go and visit other people's houses. The first thing they would ask was, "Would you like a smoke?" Then they would go to the fridge and pull out their stash of weed.

Of course, I never smoked, so I would say, "No thanks. I'll have a coffee."

It was a different way of life!

There were quite a few big towns between 20mi. and 40mi. away around which we would travel. One day, we were in a pawn shop in Grants Pass, and Ron spotted and bought a 1904 Winchester rifle, a beautiful gun. I had never fired a gun in my life but just by picking it up and feeling it, you could tell that it was spot on.

Money was always tight, as Ron was living just by selling logs or rabbits. His place in the forest was about 10mi. from the main road, and you would pass lakes and other people's properties as you were driving up there. One area we used to pass was a valley. In the bottom of the valley was a very wide river. On the odd occasion, you could spot a deer there. Every time we went to Gilligan's Butte, we would be on the lookout for a deer for food. Ron shot one, and that kept us going for quite a while. One day, I saw and shot a deer, and it hurt me afterwards to think about it. Oh no, what had I done? This deer was a beautiful thing, but we needed the food.

After a while, Ron bought this old 1958 Mack truck and started to work hauling loads. He took Paulette with him, and they didn't come back for three months! They followed the work, taking loads to wherever they needed to go, usually a couple of hundred miles. When they reached their destination, Ron would look around for another load, and that would take them off in another direction.

This left Robert and me staying at Ron's place. In the States, they have hunting seasons and permits required. This wasn't the hunting season, but we were hungry and went out one day looking for a deer. We were walking side by side up the edge of the river, and then Robert went on ahead quite a distance in front of me. I heard this shot go off, and Robert's voice shouted, "It's in the river!" I jumped into the river, which wasn't deep, just about waist height. I was looking for a deer and couldn't see anything. I shouted out to Robert that I couldn't see a deer, and he shouted back that it wasn't a deer but a salmon he had shot at! I finally spotted it and ushered it onto the bank at the far side. I then dragged it back across the river to where Robert was waiting. It weighed 30lb! Boy, did we eat well for a couple of days after that.

When we went out looking for something to eat, Robert would go ahead of me with the gun while I kept well back. We had a lucky escape one day when I heard Robert shout for me to come over to where he was by the road. As I slowly ambled up to him, I saw he was stood talking to two guys. When I reached him, I noticed there was a vehicle parked next to them, and they started asking questions about what we were doing and where we were going. It was only then that I noticed that on the side of the vehicle it said, 'Park and Game Warden'. My reply was that we were looking for a mountain lion, as we had seen tracks up on our property, which was quite a few miles further along the road. Robert had said the same, because we had truly found some tracks, but they might have been paw prints from a large dog! They didn't buy our story, and we had to eat a bit of humble pie, but eventually they let us go with a verbal warning.

While Ron and Paulette were away, I was looking after

their two children and hundreds of rabbits. The children were fine, no problem. They were about seven or eight years old, and so long as I fed and watered them and made sure they caught the school bus in the morning, they were great. The rabbits were more hard work. Having to clean out hundreds of cages and feed and water them twice a day was an ongoing full-time job. I would start when the children got off to school and then finish at about 11.30am or noon for lunch. I would start again in the afternoon and finish as the children got back from school. We survived for about three months. Sometimes, I would walk down into Cave Junction, about five miles away, and have lunch there in the middle of the day. Sometimes I would call in on a great guy called Gerry. He was a truck mechanic who had spent years in Alaska repairing trucks out there. I asked him how he had managed in the cold, where it could be 30 or 40 degrees below freezing. He said that all you did was go out and hook the wagon up to tow it back into the warehouse to work on. Gerry was a Chevy man and had three Chevrolets in his yard, a 1933, a 1941 and a 1955. He would work on them between other jobs. He also had a big barn with chain blocks and welding plants.

While I was in Cave Junction, I wrote some good songs. At lunchtime, when I had finished feeding the rabbits, I would sit and play the guitar. Sometimes, as I worked my way through other songs, a new idea would come to me. I wrote a nice one about Gerry and his Chevrolets. Walking back to the house from town one day, a song came into my head about a unicorn. It was a lovely tune, and I was searching around for bits of paper and a pen to write the words down. By the time I had made it the five miles back to the house, I had all the words down, but I'd lost the tune. I had to make up another tune to go with my lyrics, but it was a good song.

Robert was an artist. He carved wood, and he painted. One day, we were driving through a town, and he pointed out a carved Indian in a shop doorway. He told me that he had made it, and I remember thinking it was good. Robert took me to Portland, where he had a big job to do. Someone for whom he had worked previously had now bought a massive building there, and he wanted Robert's genius to sort it. It was a timber yard that had two huge Nissen huts (each about 25ft high and 40ft wide) and a store at the side. He wanted us to make the store like a Western saloon. I worked with Robert on that job, but then my skin irritation from the poison ivy got worse with the heat, so I ended up having to go back down to Cave Junction. It was about 100°F, and I was itching more than anything. Ron took me to a doctor, and I got some ointment for it. When I got back to Portland, Robert had finished painting the two Nissen huts using a cherry picker. He had painted a woodland scene with a river running through, and when the sliding doors were opened, it matched up with the other paintings. It was amazing. Robert also carved a sign to be erected at the side of the road to advertise the wood shop. It was about 20ft long and at least 10ft high. Another woodland scene was carved and painted on both sides, and it was put up with a couple of cranes and cemented into the ground. I had never seen work like it; I was speechless when I saw it. Unfortunately, I never got any photos of it.

On the next trucking trip, I went with Ron. What a fantastic experience for a Lancashire lad, trucking through the States, listening to country music, talking on the CB radio; it was like I had gone to heaven! I have always been into country music and rock and roll, and it was just magic.

On that first trip, we ended up in eastern Arizona, dropping some equipment off at a place called Snowflake. On the way back, we stopped off in Phoenix, where Ron met up with some old friends of his. Luckily, this guy had a condo he was not using, as he was staying with his partner in her house. Ron and I got to stay in this luxury apartment whilst we were in Phoenix before heading back to Cave Junction.

Our next trip was a biggie. We needed to go with a Chevy Blazer, so I drove that while Ron drove the big truck. Whilst driving through Nevada at night, it was freezing, despite having been red hot during the day. It got so cold that the steering on the truck seized up and Ron couldn't move the wheel. He managed to get the truck off the road to safety, and early the next morning we drove into the nearest town in the Blazer. We found a hardware store and had to wait until it opened up before we could buy a blowtorch. We then headed back to the truck, where we dismantled the steering block and found that water had been getting in and the whole thing was a block of solid ice! We melted it out, filled it with oil and put everything back together. Bingo, we were back on the road.

On the outskirts of Las Vegas, we had a blowout on one of the truck tyres. It was a Friday night, and, after limping into a truck stop, we found that it was a public holiday weekend so nothing would be open until Monday. Ron phoned up somebody he knew to come and collect us, which they did. Ron had lived in Vegas for a while previously and had met and married Paulette there. She used to perform as part of a duo in one of the lounge bars on the strip. As I have said, I had always been into country music, so I was listening to the radio during our journey into the city. The radio station mentioned that if you went to the Las Vegas Hotel and told them that you had been listening to their station, you would get reasonable room rates. Ron's friend dropped us at the hotel, and, lo and behold, we got a full suite for $20!

That night, I opened the curtains to see all the lights on the strip. It was extraordinary. We didn't have much money, and it was going to cost quite a bit to get the truck sorted out, so we embarked on the same course of action we had used in Sierra Leone. Ron played blackjack while I walked around for a while, then I would pass by him and pick up a load of chips. This went on for a while, but in Vegas they were a lot craftier than they had been in Sierra Leone. They used to change the croupier often, every time they saw somebody winning in fact, to try to break their stride. In the end, we won about $900. Much later on in my time in the States, we found ourselves in Vegas again and repeated this, winning about $800 that time.

This is where the story changes a bit. For some reason, Ron and I ended up in Phoenix again, and we stayed there. Ron never went back to Cave Junction, to Paulette and the children. It seemed that we got more loads out of Phoenix than anywhere else, and the truck was kept at the Phoenix truck stop. We rented an apartment nearby. I don't know what the problem was, Ron never said anything to me about it and I didn't think it was my place to interfere in his marriage. During the time I had spent with Ron and Paulette in Africa and in Cave Junction, I had never found any disharmony between them. Even when I had spent six months living in their family home with them, I had been accepted into the family, no problem. It could be that, due to the horrendous conditions through which we had lived, Ron and I had ended up as sort of brothers. The scars of what had happened to us in Africa took some time to heal, and even now, when I go through my journals from that time, it brings back the pain and the hate that I had locked away for 40 years. Doing this book has helped me tremendously to let it out, like therapy, I would think. It really used to hurt me to look at my journals and think about what I put up with and went through for nothing.

While we were in Phoenix and I was looking for something to do, I found a job at a scrapyard. It wasn't for vehicles but for all kinds of engineering equipment, like big tanks, boilers and all sorts. I was there welding and repairing all kinds of stuff. I had a young lad helping me called Bob Davis. His dad was called Rusty Davis and was one of the first Marlboro men (American cigarettes) from the 1960s. He was a country singer, and I met him when he was touring in the area. Similar to the hippy chiropractor I had seen in the Oregon mountains, Rusty saw me and said, "Your back looks out," then grabbed me and cracked it! Bob drove one of those enormous monster trucks like the original Bigfoot. It was an ordinary Ford pick-up truck made high using special shock absorbers and big truck wheels. I got in it once, and it wobbled all over the place. Bob told me that in the winter he would drive out of Phoenix Valley to the hillier forest regions and spend the weekend helping pull out people who were stuck in snowdrifts. He used to make quite a bit of money at it. Bob asked me to help him make a friend's pick-up truck into a monster truck. I welded brackets under the chassis to take the large shock absorbers.

Phoenix as a town had grown and spread out so fast that they hadn't put any drainage systems in place along with the rapid building. Instead, they had made a high camber to the roads so that, on the rare occasions when it rained heavily, excess water would run down gullies at the side. On one particular day, I went in our battered old pick-up truck to exchange empty oxyacetylene bottles for full ones. The tailgate on the pick-up was so battered that it was really very hard to close, so we never did. The oxy centre was about five miles down the road. It was a noisy place, with people clanging bottles about and what have you. I loaded up with my full bottles, paid and set off back to the scrapyard. On arriving back and extracting the bottles from the pick-up to the store, I realised I was a bottle short. I knew they had all been there before I had left the centre. Oh my God, had one fallen out on the journey!? If the valve had been knocked off when it landed, it would have been like a torpedo going off; there was so much pressure inside. I drove back down the road looking for catastrophic damage. I was terrified of the consequences, and my heart was in my mouth. I didn't come across any damage, so I slowly drove back into the centre and went up to the chargehand, feeling very embarrassed.

I said, "Sorry to trouble you, but has anyone found an oxygen bottle lying around?"

Well, the guy blew his top, shouting, "It's you, you *******!"

It must have happened as I drove out of the centre and then up onto the high camber of the road. The bottle had slid out of the back of the pick-up and I hadn't heard it because of the noise of the centre. I had made the same trip umpteen times before without incident. They made me tie it in safe and then struggle to close the tailgate, which I had to borrow a hammer to do. Strict orders about safety were then issued to me. Later on, screw caps were introduced over the valves to make them safer. At least the experience made me sort out the tailgate so that it closed properly after that! It also made me realise the devastation I could have caused by not being diligent.

One day, much later on, I was working in the workshop on the outskirts of Phoenix, and as usual I had the radio on playing country music. Suddenly, a warning came over the radio about bad weather coming in. It was about 10am, and I looked up into the usual clear-blue sky. There were no dark clouds anywhere. A bit later, another warning came on. This time when I looked up, I noticed a black line on the horizon. I had never seen anything like this: the whole horizon was just black, and it was slowly coming closer and closer. The radio stations always had a chopper in the skies looking for traffic jams and advising people to take alternative routes. They started to advise people to leave work now or else they wouldn't get home at all. By this time, the black sky of the storm was very close. Above me I could still see the chopper, and I could hear the radio man inside it broadcasting and sounding really panicked, because they were being buffeted about. He was saying, "Get me down, now!"

Then the rains came. I had been in some heavy storms in Africa at the height of the rainy season, but this eclipsed anything I had ever been through before. The radio was now advising people to stay where they were until at least 8pm that night. I hunkered down in the cabin in the workshop and just listened to the radio; there was nothing else I could do. I think it started to ease off at about 6pm and stopped raining by about 7pm. I didn't leave the yard until closer to 9pm, because I knew the roads would still be flooded.

Whilst I was working in the scrapyard, there was one particular job which we were rushing to finish. I was using a pedestal grinder to grind a bit of pipe. In England, there is glass or plastic which comes over to shield your eyes from sparks, and you have guards coming up to the wheels. This had neither. You would never have been allowed to use it in England. I was in a hurry, and as I was holding the pipe, it sucked my fingers in. I lost the end of one of my fingers and another two were so badly damaged that I haven't been able to straighten them since. It was a mess. They took me to the nearest hospital, which turned out to be the county hospital where they catered for prisoners, Mexicans, people with no money etc. A normal hospital wouldn't have admitted me without insurance. At this county hospital, they sat me at a sink and gave me a nail brush and what looked like a cardboard container of Vim.

They said, "Sorry, we've run out of stuff to get the dirt off, and we can't do anything until your hands are clean."

My hands were black, and I had to start cleaning them with the Vim and the brush while blood was spurting everywhere. It was so painful. I scrubbed and scrubbed for about an hour until I couldn't do any more. Finally, they came, patched me up and sent me home. That night, the pain came, and I was on the floor curled up in agony. They hadn't given me any painkillers or anything. Luckily, a neighbour came by and saw how much I was suffering. They gave me a couple of glasses of Jim Beam and Coke! It helped, and I have liked it ever since; mind you, I prefer Bacardi and Coke now.

They operated on both my hands a few days later. The fingers on my left hand were pinned back to my wrist for quite a while. Of course, not only did this put me off work, but it also knackered my guitar playing. Even today, my fingers get so sore and are so sensitive that I struggle to write with a normal pen. When I started playing again, I would always drop the guitar pick, because I had lost feeling, and sometimes I couldn't get the chords with my right hand. When I think back to the poor lad I met in Cave

Junction who lost all his fingers and thumbs cutting timber, I know that I was lucky my injuries weren't much worse. After treating me, the hospital demanded about $3,000, so I had to find a lawyer who would take my case claiming against the scrapyard. Of course, they wanted a quarter of the price on a contingency. If they won, I would have to pay them; if they lost, I didn't have to pay them anything. In the end, they won, and I got $10,000, from which I had to pay the hospital and the lawyer's fees. That left me with about $4,000.

A short while after the accident, I had a funny experience. Although it wasn't funny at the time, it was quite serious. I was out one night in a bar and got friendly with a crowd of people. They were a mixed bunch of a similar age to me. I had a couple of beers, and we were all having a good time. At the end of the night, one of the girls asked me if I could drop her back to where she was staying. Being the gentleman that I am, I agreed. We jumped in my car, and I asked the question, "Where are we going?" to which she replied, "Sun City." I had heard of Sun City; it was a massive retirement town for rich people. It had its own golf courses, hospitals, cinemas etc. It seems that this girl lived somewhere else in Arizona but was visiting her parents in Sun City. The locals called people who lived there 'snowbirds', meaning that people with out-of-town plates on their cars had only come there to get out of the winter snows. Phoenix Valley is known for year-round sun and warm temperatures. From what I remember, it never got colder than 70°F, even in winter. Even Ron and I had been called snowbirds, because the Chevy Blazer had Oregon plates on it.

Sun City is roughly 30mi. from the centre of Phoenix, and the bar we were at was on the outskirts. To people there, a distance of 20mi. or so is nothing. As we arrived in Sun City,

I could see that all the houses were very posh, and it took some time to find where this girl was staying. Meanwhile, I thought that we were being followed, as I could just make out lights in my rear-view mirror. I then realised that we were being tailed by a patrol car. Luckily, we were not far from the house we were looking for, and the girl was giving me directions. When she said, "Right at this roundabout," I went the wrong way around the roundabout! Finally, she told me to pull into a driveway, and I found I was facing a large double garage. The girl got a fob out of her purse, and when she pressed it, the doors started going up. I drove into the garage, and she pressed the button again, which made the doors close behind us, right onto the bonnet of the police car! She had to lift the door up again, and that police officer was not a happy bunny, especially when I told him one of his lights was out! He was saying a lot of not very nice words, and the girl was saying, "Can you please turn your lights and siren off? You're upsetting the neighbours." He was not pleased whatsoever and took me outside to make me walk the line. That is hard enough to do when you have not had a drink, but I managed it. Then he got me to stand with my arms outstretched and slowly bring my finger in to touch my nose. I did it a few times and passed that test too. Then the officer put a few coins on the ground. I knew there was no way I could pick them up with my hands after the accident, so I had to explain to him what had happened to me.

He finally relented, but by this time the girl's parents had woken up and had come to see what all the noise was about. They helped calm the situation down and pacify the policeman, who was still not happy. Eventually, he let me off, saying, "I'm watching you," before driving away. With this being such a prestigious area, Sun City had patrol cars cruising around 24/7 looking out for drivers like me – ones who went round roundabouts the wrong way! The girl's dad said that I could sleep on their couch that night, because otherwise they might have been waiting to arrest me as I left. I was glad, but I was out of there the next morning as soon as it was light. I struggled to find my way out of Sun City, but I managed it and got back to Phoenix. I never went back to that bar, and, luckily, I also never saw that girl again. That was one close call.

When I was off work after my accident, it got to Christmastime and Ron was out on the road. What do you do on a lonely Christmas? I remembered back to what I did in Sierra Leone, when my two friends and I had gone around giving people those small token presents wrapped in newspaper. I then recalled that we had kept half a sack of pinto beans from one of the trips we did, the type you make chilli out of. I went around knocking on the doors of all the apartments in the development in which we were living. When someone answered the door, I would offer them a bowlful of beans. It made me a lot of new friends.

It was while I was in Phoenix that I met up with Big John Smith again. As I said previously, I had given John my last $100 bill, my emergency money, and left him under house arrest in Sierra Leone. When I next arrived back in Freetown, John had gone and nobody knew how he had gotten away. John had given me an address of a bar called Old West Trails on the outskirts of the city when we were back in Sierra Leone, so I found the bar and asked for him, but of course they said they had never heard of him. I told them that we had been in Africa together, and I realised that, due to John's business, they were checking me out whilst separately someone was contacting him. Finally, John arrived. We had a big celebration, and then he explained to me how he had escaped.

I mentioned before how I had gone to see Mickey the diamond dealer and made him promise to try to help John while I was up country. Mickey obviously did this, contacting John's company back in America and arranging for them to send John a ticket out. Mickey brought the ticket to John and then promised that he would come back and collect him the next day in time to take him to the airport. John carried on as usual, heading to the beach for a swim as he did every day, telling the guard what he was doing and walking off wearing his T-shirt, shorts and flip-flops, with a towel over his shoulder. Mickey had arranged to meet John a mile down the beach so that nobody would see them. John got into Mickey's old Mercedes and they set off, but they had not got far down the road when the car conked out. They were pushing the car into a restaurant car park when another car drew up alongside them. It was the police inspector who'd had John under arrest back at headquarters.

He said, "Mr Smith, what are you doing away from the hotel? You're under house arrest."

John replied, "This gentleman broke down, so I volunteered to help push his car."

The inspector told John that he had better get himself back to the hotel, as the police were advancing with their investigation, and then he and his wife headed into the restaurant. John realised that they were coming to throw him in jail, so he really started to panic. Luckily, a taxi drew up to drop off its passengers at the restaurant. The driver was one that Mickey used regularly. I had seen this African a couple of times, and I didn't like him. He was very surly, and he wouldn't look you in the eyes – very shifty. He turned them down flat, saying, "I'm not taking him." Everybody knew the story of the trouble John was in, and he didn't want to get involved. Mickey had some bribing to do, and the taxi driver finally relented but insisted that John had to get into the car boot. Think about it: it was a three-hour journey to the airport, in a confined space, in the heat, squashed in alongside the tins of oil and all sorts that were also in the boot.

The taxi driver dropped John at the entrance of the airport, and then John had to hide while Mickey went and paid the airport tax. Mickey passed John the ticket, and then he got back in the taxi and headed off. When the last call for passengers came, John dashed into the queue. Don't forget that his passport name was not John Smith, it was Norman something or other, and his photo looked quite different. He was to fly from Sierra Leone to London and then get a connection to the States. Whilst they were waiting to take off, all of a sudden, the plane was surrounded by the army. John started to worry again, thinking that they were going to drag him off the plane. After a short delay, a plane arrived from the National Diamond Company (that's why the army was there), and then John's flight was allowed to leave. Phew!

John managed to get to London OK, and then he had to go through passport control again. Don't forget, he was still wearing the same beach clothes and had nothing else with him. He was pulled to one side by authorities to have his ticket checked, which again made him think that his number was up. It seems that in Sierra Leone someone was forging tickets, and they just wanted to verify that his ticket was registered properly. When they saw that it was, they let him through.

On the connecting flight to the USA, John was sitting next to a Texan who had been working on the North Sea oil rigs. This guy took one look at John and said, "Buddy, I think you need a wash or something." He opened his briefcase and gave John a shirt and pants that he carried as spares. He told John, "Go and sort yourself out," which he did. John was grateful, and then he told the guy his story. As they parted, this guy gave John his card and told him that if he needed a job, he could call him. Somewhere along the journey back to Phoenix, John lost the guy's card, which he explained to me when I asked why he hadn't got in touch with the guy again.

That was how John escaped from Sierra Leone, but there were also other stories about him. He would hardly tell you anything about his past himself. Even if you asked him directly, he wouldn't be drawn into speaking about it much. One night, I was at a party that some friends of John's were having. I got talking to one guy, and he said to me, "Anyone who has saved John's life is my friend for life." Of course, I didn't know what he was on about, but I suppose John must have told him about Sierra Leone. This guy went on to tell me what had happened to him and John one day. They had been working together and had finished their day's work by lunchtime. They had decided to go to the Old West Trails. As you went through the doors of the bar, you entered a big square room with the oblong bar in the middle. Around the edges of the room were jukeboxes, one-armed bandits, pool tables and such. As John and this guy had entered the bar, they had realised that something was wrong. The place was empty except for two men and the lady behind the bar, all of whom were standing at one end of the bar where one of the tills was. As they had shouted for some service, these two men had turned around and they had seen that one had a pistol and the other a sawn-off shotgun. The men had told John and his friend to empty their pockets. Straight away, John had told them that he'd left his wallet in his pick-up. His friend, knowing John well, had just followed his lead and said, "Well, you've got all the money, John." The robbers had then made them go outside to the pick-up. John's friend had known that John would do something as they reached the door. He had gone first, with the pistol-wielding robber behind him, and then John had followed, with Mr Shotgun behind him. As they had reached the door, John's friend had dived to the floor. John had spun around, grabbed the shotgun and hit the guy over the head with it. Then he had spun back and fired it at the other guy, blasting him. That was it, one robber had been knocked out and the other dead. The police had come to try to sort it out, and it had been classed as a justifiable homicide.

One day, I was driving through one of the small towns that made up the Phoenix area when John pointed out a restaurant to me. He said that it had previously been a bar he had known. As I pestered him with questions, he finally opened up to me. John used to frequent this bar, and one day when he had arrived there, he had noticed the bartender was looking very glum. He had then told John that someone had called in and demanded protection money of $500 a week, but there was no chance he had enough to cover that every week. They had given him the time when the man was due to come looking to collect his first payment. John had told the bartender not to worry, that he would be there. On that night, John arrived early and explained to the bartender, "If I say 'move', you need to dive out the way." Finally, the gangster came in, and he and John recognised each other. The guy was a mixed-race

Apache and a really bad person. He asked the bartender what his answer was to paying the protection money, and the bartender said no. The gangster then said, "OK, well you know what's coming." He turned and walked back towards the door, and, as he reached it, he turned around to start shooting. John shouted, "Move!" The bartender dived one way, and John shot the gangster. When the police arrived, they went through the crime scene and recognised the gangster from wanted posters. They said to John that he had done them a big favour! Justifiable homicide again.

At one time, John was dating somebody at the apartments where we lived, and I was seeing him more and more often. Then I realised that I hadn't seen him for a couple of weeks and started to get worried. I phoned him up and asked where he was. He could hardly speak to reply, so I asked him what was wrong. It seemed that he had been set up. Somebody had told him there was a job for him and given him an address. When he had got there, there had been a gang waiting for him. They had battered him with all sorts, and he was a real mess. I told him that I would come to his house to collect him. He said, "No, don't come anywhere near. There's sure to be somebody watching all the time, and then they'll be after you. Keep away; I'll be all right." Fortunately, after a while, he recovered.

Back to trucking, and Ron meanwhile had managed to get a contract taking large earth-moving vehicles from Salt Lake City to a place called College Station, just outside Houston in Texas. From Phoenix, this was a 4,000mi. round trip. Both the tractor unit and the body unit, when loaded on low-loaders, was each approximately 14ft high by 14ft wide. With them being so big, we needed escort vehicles and signs everywhere to alert other people on the road.

That was my job in the Chevy Blazer: to be the front escort vehicle. God knows how I found my way, because we didn't have satnav back then! Every state we passed through had different laws. The worst one was Texas itself, where we were not allowed to drive these loads on the weekend. Also, we were not allowed on the motorways and instead had to take the A and B roads, which was extremely dangerous. A lot of the small towns we passed through had traffic lights strung across the street, which was a problem for us given the height of the body units we were trying to drive underneath. One of the other journeys we made was delivering a load of gypsum. Our destination was just a mile over the state line, but nevertheless we were made to pay a large fuel tax for entering the state.

I enjoyed the trucking lifestyle. It was like being on one big lifetime holiday. We stopped at truck stops and motels, and it was a magical time. Mind you, we had problems with highway patrol and state troopers. I lost count of the times we were pulled over for all kinds of reasons. As I have said before, each state we passed through had their own rules governing the whys and wherefores. In New Mexico, we had to have two escort cars, one in front and one behind. We had to hire a company from New Mexico, and, believe it or not, they were called Apache Escorts! All the other states only required one escort vehicle. After a couple of visits, we asked if we could hire just the signs. The conditions were that the escorts had to be registered in New Mexico, so, by hiring their signs, which were registered there, we got away with it. We always took two cars with us from then on, but I think Ron stopped sending the fee to them for every time we went through. On one journey, we were passing through Albuquerque, heading for the truck stop there to fill up with diesel. By the time we had pulled into the truck stop, we were surrounded by more police than I had ever seen. There was the highway patrol, state troopers, local police and some others I can't even remember. There were about 10 officers all around us. It seemed that we had been spotted by the Apache Escort company, and they had phoned for back-up. It took a lot of sorting out. Ron had to wire someone to borrow some money to pay off the fines, and Apache Escorts took their signs back! We were escorted through New Mexico, but at least nobody was arrested that time.

As I mentioned, we were not allowed to drive through Texas at weekends. This was tough for us, as our deadline to be at College station was always 5pm Monday night. It would take two or three days to go through Texas, as the maximum speed was 50mph then. We always struggled to get to Texas for Thursday or Friday, and it was usually Saturday morning as we were entering the state. Luckily, Ron had a good rapport with the officer who ran the entry port where we crossed into the state. Of course, we had to pay to get in, and he would have the permits ready for us, which he usually backdated to Friday. The fella understood the problems and setbacks of the road and was a good guy. The entry port closed at lunchtime on Saturday, and, sometimes, if we were late, he would leave the permits there for us, and Ron would always pay him later. One particular time, we were late, and we picked up the permits at the entry port. We carried on sneaking along the A and B roads, past the outskirts of towns. Then, on the Sunday morning, we were spotted by a state trooper. Well, he was not happy. He pulled us over and walked around the truck (there was just one truck on this trip) and the two escort cars. Ron wasn't on this job; it was me and a hired driver who had his wife and baby with him. I was driving the front escort and the wife was driving the rear escort. The officer threw his book at the truck driver and said, "Take your pick of the fines in there, you've probably broken just about every rule going."

It was then that a realisation hit me: I remembered that I didn't have an American licence, which could mean a prison sentence. I jumped out of the Chevy Blazer, sneaked around to the rear escort car and jumped into it. I planned to claim I had been there all along and that the guy who had been driving the front car must have run away. Luckily, the officer was a good guy who took pity on us and let us away with the lowest fine he could, which was $300. This was early Sunday morning, and we now had to park up until Monday. We had a nice day out, found a motel to go and sleep in and then left again at about 5am on Monday morning. We tore through Texas as best we could and got to College station just before 6pm, and they let us into the yard.

I did arrange for my old UK licence to be sent out to me in the States, and whenever I produced it, it caused a few head scratches. The US police just couldn't make head nor tail of it. All those alphabetised categories really confused them, and I always got away with it no matter what I was driving!

On some of the journeys, I came across some strange people. In Texas, we had to use roads which were not fit for big trucks with wide loads. Most times, we would be covering both lanes. On one journey, I came up behind an elderly couple dawdling along, straddling the centre line of the road. I tooted the horn and flashed my lights but got no reaction. It was quiet, and luckily there were no other cars coming the other way. I drove alongside and put my window down. I told them we had a big truck coming through, but they just ignored me. I went past and used the CB radio to tell the truck that they were ignoring me. The driver said, "Leave it to me." He drew up right behind them, virtually touching their back bumper, and then pulled the air horn. Well, the car just flew off the road into a ditch! I would have liked to have seen the look on the driver's face when he glanced in his rear-view mirror and saw the truck right there.

On another journey, we were coming off a hill and onto a bridge that had just enough room for one vehicle. We had been on this bridge before, which was about half a mile long and crossed a massive lake. Usually, I had to race way ahead across the bridge to stop any oncoming traffic. This particular day, I was across the bridge with the lights flashing and was standing there waving red flags. A car drove past me giving me the finger! He couldn't yet see the bridge, as the road curved, and was travelling fast. He got about a quarter of the way across before he saw the truck coming towards him. He must have broken the speed limit going backwards and ended up in a ditch too! I bet he had to go and change his trousers after that too!

On one of the deliveries, Ron's younger brother, Robert, was driving the truck. He was six feet four in height too. Ron had two older other brothers too, also both six feet four, and their dad was the same. As we were coming back through New Mexico, we stopped at the truck stop at El Paso. Anywhere we stopped, we would look on the noticeboard for any other jobs that were going on that route. Rob noticed that someone was looking to ship a big D8 Caterpillar tractor, which weighed about 30tn, to Colorado. Of course, we took the job, which would be about 600mi. extra for us, and then about 700mi. back to Phoenix, coming through the Four Corners area. The Chevy was put at the front of the low loader, with the D8 behind it. Four Corners is where Utah, Arizona, Colorado and New Mexico all meet at one point. The trip over to the South Fork area of Colorado took us over Wolf Creek Pass. What a journey that was – a real white-knuckle ride. There is a famous song about this pass called Wolf Creek Pass. It's quite a funny song by a guy called CW McCall, the same guy who sang Convoy. In the song, the narrator finished in downtown Pagosa Springs – that was the end we started at, heading towards South Fork.

This pass is nearly 11,000ft high, and it was a nightmare to drive. When we had been going for a while, Rob said, "Pete, nip out and open the spare fuel tank." With the incline of the road, we weren't getting the fuel through, and the truck was struggling. On my side of the truck, there was one tank, and on the driver's side there were two. Luckily, the spare tank is near to the cab. I told Rob to pull over and I would jump out to open it. He replied, "Sorry, I can't stop or we'll never be able to pull away again with this load on." He told me to jump out and do it while the vehicle was still moving. These trucks are high, so I had to jump out, land on the road, then run like crazy to get in front of the truck and across to the driver's side. Once there, I had to run alongside and time a dive onto the tank, which lay between the cab and the wheels. I reached under, with my legs dangling, and opened the valve to the spare tank. I then threw myself back off, away from the wheels, and ran like crazy back across in front of the truck. Back at the passenger side, I then had to leap up to grab the cab door and get my feet in the footwell. The whole time, Rob was probably doing about 10–15mph. That was a close one!

As we were getting near to the top of the pass, it was getting dark. As we came down the other side, it was pitch black, steep and horrendous. The truck didn't have power steering or power brakes. It only had what was called a Jake brake (Jacob's brake), which put compression on the pistons when you take your foot off the pedal. We were going downhill with all this weight on, so even when you took your foot off the truck, it was still moving. Rob ended up being stood up while driving, standing on the brake to try to slow the truck down. We could see the lights twinkling far below us. Holy shit! Rob kept saying, "Oh, my arms are aching. Oh, my legs are aching now!" It was a nightmare! It was 43mi. along the pass, and I think nowadays there are tunnels which have been built through some parts of it, especially on the bad curves.

When we got down off the mountain and into the first bit of civilisation we saw, we found a phone box and dialled the number we had for where the delivery was supposed to go. It was midnight by this time, and the guy on the other end of the line gave us directions. It wasn't far: he just said to turn left, and he would be waiting at the top of the hill. The hill he mentioned was another mountain, with just a dirt road wide enough for a car! There were no lights, just whatever moonlight there was, plus the truck headlights. Every time we took a left-hand bend, the back end of the truck hung over the edge of the road. Luckily, we had a searchlight on top of the cab, and I would shout to alert Rob. We finally got to the top, where it flattened out a bit, and we met the guy. He was pleased to see the D8 arrive. We then asked, "How are we going to get it off?" and he replied, "Well, I don't know." We shone the searchlight around and spotted a bit of a built-up edge that was higher than the road. We drove over to it and managed to get the D8 off without doing any damage, but it was scary.

Then we had to turn the truck around to head back down, again with me shining the light around and shouting out when the truck started to overhang. It took a while, but we finally got down off the road. I looked at my watch and it was 3am! It had taken us nearly three hours to get up and down this 'hill'. We only drove on another 100yd before we were stopped by the police, who basically dragged Rob out of the driver's seat. I just climbed into the bunk bed behind the cab and fell fast asleep. The next thing I knew, the curtains were pulled back and a torch and a gun were pointed in my face. A voice was saying, "Get your ass out here now, boy." I got out and was put up against the side of the truck with my legs apart, being searched. I didn't know what the hell was going on, but it turned out they thought we had been up on the mountain shooting deer. All truckers carry guns with them, and Rob had one with him, which wasn't registered in Colorado. His gun was registered in Farmington, New Mexico, which was where he lived and where he was an honorary sheriff. I tried to tell the police that we had been delivering a D8, and I tried to give them the phone number of the guy to whom we had delivered it, but they were having none of it. They seemed to think that it was more likely we had gone deer hunting with a big low loader! It took a while, but they finally let us go, after confiscating Rob's gun (no doubt they would later let him have it back for a small fee). They followed us to the edge of the county and onto a main highway. As soon as we crossed over, we pulled in at the side of the road and Rob climbed into the back. He was knackered and instantly fell asleep, while I slept in the front seat. That mountain is in the middle of the Great Divide, which is part of the Rockies. The name means that it divides the great rivers of the States from joining the Atlantic and Pacific oceans.

The first time I met a bunch of bikers, they were not die-hard Hells Angels but were close to it. One night, I was in a bar on the outskirts of Phoenix having my first beer of the night when the bartender realised I was English.

He shouted out, "I've got an Englishman here; who wants him?"

A shout went up from this bunch of bikers, "We'll have him!"

I couldn't back down even though I wanted to, so I grabbed my beer and sauntered over to them. They got me a chair, and straight away we were all the best of friends. All except one. This guy was obviously of Irish descent, and he kept on about the IRA etc. There was no way I was going to fall for that one. I simply evaded every question he asked me, and he finally gave up. He had probably never even been to Ireland. In fact, my younger half-sister, Ann, was in Harrods at the time of its bombing. Luckily, she was at the other end of the shop when the explosion happened.

We carried on drinking and talking, and we had a super time. By closing time, they were proud to show me their bikes and choppers. They were all 1950s Harleys and things like that – beautiful bikes. One story I heard, which I know to be true even though I didn't see it myself, happened in a biker's bar on the outskirts of Phoenix. A drunk drew up in his pick-up and went in demanding a beer. The bikers took one look at him, clobbered him and threw him out. The drunk got up, and as he staggered towards his pick-up, he noticed all the bikes parked in a row outside. Of course, he proceeded to drive over all the bikes. The bikers spotted him doing this and all piled outside with every gun that they could lay their hands on. They blasted the drunk and his pick-up to pieces. When the police arrived, there was nobody to arrest, no guns to be found and the bartender said he hadn't seen or heard anything. The only thing the police could find was that some of the bikes weren't registered in that state. This poor drunk worked as an electrician at a massive power plant somewhere outside the Phoenix area. I think everybody who worked there was called an electrician, and there were over a hundred of them, all wanting revenge for what had happened to their colleague. In time, everybody forgot about the incident; the electricians had been waiting for the dust to settle before they made their move. Months after the event, they struck. They came with 14lb hammers, picks, baseball bats, you name it. They flattened the bar, the bikes and whoever was inside the bar at the time. There was no more biker bar after that. Revenge with a vengeance.

The last time I saw a full-blooded Hells Angels biker, he was stood in the doorway of a 7-Eleven store near where I was working. I would usually call into the store and take home something to eat and maybe the odd beer. He was standing there in all his colours with his hands on an automatic pistol, which was holstered in his belt. He looked like he wanted someone to call him out. I just squeezed past him while trying to look nonchalant. He was still there when I came out, and I made a fast exit.

As we got into 1983, I started to spend less time on the road and more time staying in Phoenix to repair the trailers, which were breaking often due to the weight they were bearing. We had quite a big house by this time, with quite a few bedrooms for the various truck drivers who would stay over. One of the big rooms had a few single beds in it, but I had a small room to myself. Ron had a new girlfriend, and

I didn't get on with her. I thought she was weird, and she didn't like me at all. In fact, she hated me and kept trying to get rid of me. Whether she was jealous of my friendship with Ron I don't know. She wanted me out of my bedroom and sleeping in a single bed in a room with the others. One particular day, she was out on a trip driving the escort vehicle when the convoy stopped somewhere for a rest. They spotted what they thought was a small sheep running wild, but it turned out to be the cutest little dog, with twigs, grass and all sorts stuck in its curly white hair. It had either run off from its owner or perhaps had been kicked out by someone who didn't like it. At that point, I was living somewhere else, looking after a friend's house while he was on a long touring holiday. The first time I called at the house after they brought the dog home, I was appalled at how badly the dog was being treated, mainly by her. She was the one at home most of the time, and she left the dog outside the whole time, even in 100° heat. It only had scraps to live on and no water. I just picked the dog up and took it away with me. I gave him the name Pooch. I looked after him properly, but he always seemed to me to be a really paranoid animal. If anyone opened a car door, he would run and jump in straight away, no matter whose vehicle it was. Luckily, Ron got rid of that girlfriend before too long!

As the trucking business started to expand, we took over an area of land on which we had space to repair the trucks. We took on the guy who rented it, Jim, to work with us. The constant weight of the earthmoving equipment meant that repairing the trailers became a full-time job. We also employed an African American called James. He was a big guy; he made Mr T look like a small lad. The truck tyres were heavy, but he used to pick them up and throw them about like they were nothing.

One day, James was messing about with some steel, and I said, "James, what are you doing?"

He told me that he was going to make a barbecue for Thanksgiving. I told him to leave it to me and Jim and that we would make it for him. Well, we made a really good one out of a 25gal. drum and put wheels on it and everything. It was the Rolls-Royce of barbecues! James was so grateful that he invited Jim and me to have ribs and chicken with him at his house. That Saturday, I took a case of beer, Jim took a bottle of Jim Beam and we found this shack where James lived. You've heard the saying 'the wrong side of the tracks', well, this whole area was definitely on the wrong side of the tracks. Not to worry, we went in. I had brought my guitar and mouth organ with me, assuming that the people there would know all the blues songs. Bingo, I looked at James's record collection and every one was blues. We had a great time. It wasn't a big house, but it was full of James's relations and friends. I never saw any women, but I guess they were outside doing the barbecuing and enjoying the party in their own way. James had disappeared by this time.

All of a sudden, this black guy came in covered in bling: all chains and rings just like in Miami Vice. He was from the West Indies, and, with me being English, he thought we were very similar. He came over to me and started chatting. I thought he was a bit weird and not exactly my cup of tea, but fair enough. Then, gradually, the atmosphere began to change and get a lot worse. Jim was on the other side of the room in the middle of a bunch of other guys, all of whom had been really friendly. From having a great time, suddenly the atmosphere was really bad, and I didn't know what was going on. Suddenly, one of the guys with whom we had been having a good time walked through the door holding a sawn-off shotgun, pointed it at the West Indian guy and said, "I'm gonna blow that mother fucker's ass off!"

I looked at Jim, he looked at me, I picked up my guitar and then, just like a cartoon character, I ran around the back of the couch and out of the door, with Jim following two seconds behind me! If that gun went off in that small room, everyone was going to get a piece. I then asked Jim what the hell had gone on. He said that the West Indian must have said he was carrying a gun and that he would shoot anyone who was in his way. The guy with the shotgun must have thought, "Well, mine's bigger than his." It seemed that this West Indian guy had been dating another guy's daughter. Nobody liked him, especially since he called the rest of them "slaves" and said that he was "a true black", which was nonsense, as everybody knew we filled the West Indies with slaves to grow tobacco and sugar cane. Luckily, no shots were fired while Jim and I were there. We didn't see James again, so we never found out what happened. That was so weird.

I had been in America since 1981, and on 31st December 1982, my visa ran out. We were having such a good time over the Christmas and New Year period that I forgot all about it. It was only when I looked at my passport a short while later that I realised. What to do? Plan B. I thought that if I could get into Canada for a while, I could then come back to the States with another six-month visa. I had tried to get a green card but to no avail. In that period, even England was in a bit of a depression, as was the States.

Ron wrote a letter for me to present to companies in Canada about our transport company, Trans Global Services, to try to get us some more business. I caught a truck ride most of the way, up as far as Seattle, after which I jumped on a Greyhound bus heading for Vancouver. Of course, when I got to the border on the Canadian side, we all had to get out and take our baggage with us. I also, as usual, had my guitar with me. I joined the queue, and when it got to my turn, I handed over my ticket and passport. I probably looked like a long-haired hippy or redneck. The guy behind the counter gave me a really hard time. He questioned me about why I was there, where I was staying (obviously nowhere), how much money I had (about US$60). He told me I didn't have enough money, and I replied that I also had about £300 on me, but he wouldn't have that. Every time I came up with something, he just shot me down. By this time, everybody else had gone through and got on the bus.

Finally, he said, "Your visa has run out. You'll have to go over to the American border post and sort it out with them."

I picked up my ticket, passport, guitar and my small bag and ambled over to the other side. I explained to them that my visa had expired about six or seven days before, and they just told me to go and sit down. It was a nice place, with plenty of seats, tables and magazines. I sat there for half an hour or so, and when I looked up, the tallest guy I had ever seen (about seven feet) had come into the reception. He walked over to me and showed me my passport, asking if it was mine. When I confirmed that it was, he said, "Pick up your stuff, boy, and follow me." I noticed his uniform said that he was border patrol. We went outside, he opened the boot of a car and I put my belongings inside. He opened the back door of the car and I got in. I soon realised that I was in big trouble. There was mesh on all the car windows and no handles on the insides of the doors. There was a big partition separating me from the driver.

When we arrived at the border patrol building, I got my stuff out of the car and the tall man spoke through an intercom to get access. Inside, I got the biggest third-degree interrogation, lasting about three hours. Luckily, the story I told coincided with my passport, but at the end of it the man simply said, "I'm just going to have to get you deported."

Wow! That was the worst thing I could possibly hear. The man left me, saying that he was going to sort out the paperwork. I was devastated. I think I must have prayed to everybody and everything I could think of. When he finally came back, he said, "I'm going to extend your visa until the end of the month to get yourself sorted out." What a relief! I collected my gear, threw it in his boot and jumped back into his car. He drove me to the Greyhound bus stop. There were quite a few people waiting there. We drew up, and, as I got out, the officer said, "Get your stuff, boy. I don't want to see you again." Well, the people at the bus stop scurried away like the parting of the Red Sea! As I went to the ticket office to get myself back to Seattle, I really felt like a criminal.

Whilst waiting at the truck stop for a ride back to Phoenix, I met the real-life Santa Claus. It was evening time and quite a few truckers and I were sitting around drinking coffee and swapping stories. This guy was a trucker with silver wavy hair down to his shoulders, a wavy silver beard, twinkling eyes and little glasses. How nobody had ever signed him up to star in Santa movies I'll never know! Honestly, he was the living image of Santa Claus. On the way back to Phoenix, I managed to stop off where Ray lived. You will remember how Ray and Tom had left Sierra Leone along with Paulette when our real trouble had started there. His place was on the California–Oregon border, and he was a great guy. Just like Mickey the diamond dealer and his business partner,

Ray had been through the Vietnam War. I apologised for having left the guitar he had given me in Sierra Leone when I had fled the country, and he understood. We had a good time reminiscing.

I made it back to Phoenix, and then, within the one-month deadline that the border patrol officer had given me, I returned to England at the end of January 1983. It was during the time that I was back home that I met up with Shirley again at a dance hall.

I'll let Shirley tell you this bit:

It was Saturday night, and I was out with my friend, Carol. We were going to a nightclub in Ribchester. This was about a 25-minute drive away, and I felt tired, so I suggested that instead we go to Lah De Dahs, a nightclub near where we were in Accrington. This we did, and as I was walking off the dance floor, a hand reached out and grabbed me. It was Pete.

My first words were, "Oh Pete North, look at the state of you!" His hair was down to his shoulders. "What happened to you?"

He couldn't remember my name but remembered that I'd been in his life for a short while in the past.

We chatted for a while, and he asked to take me out the following night. Pete told me he was back from America for a few weeks, and during that time we went out a lot and became quite close. When he went back to the States, we wrote and spoke on the phone. I was thrilled to bits when he asked me to go over when school finished in July. Strange how things work out – I wasn't meant to go to Ribchester that night; instead, Pete and I were finally meant to get together!

Back to me, and before I had left the States at the end of January 1983, we had initiated Plan C. Ron wrote another letter for me (to help me get back into America). It told of how I had been drumming up business in England and Europe for Trans Global Services and was coming back into the States after a short holiday back home. Well, that was another mistake. Landing in the States, I joined a queue to get through passport control. I was behind a gentleman, and, when it was his turn, the African American lady didn't half give him a hard time. It was just like when I was trying to get into Canada. The poor guy didn't stand a chance, and God knows what happened to him. He didn't get into the States. I had been going through Plan C and Ron's letter. Well, when I approached the lady, I just bottled it and said I was here for a holiday. Wow! She was as nice as ninepence, stamped my passport and just waved me through. It was hard to believe it. Another six months! The gods must have been smiling on me again.

When I got back to Phoenix, I met up with a guy called Tom, who lived in the same apartments as us. He was from upstate New York, and I became really good friends with him. By trade, he was a cylindrical grinder, real heavy-duty stuff. He worked locally, and when he was laid off by his company, Ron gave him a job in our office. He spent his time phoning around and getting loads for our truck drivers. The company of Trans Global Services was like an agency or brokers really. After our contract to move earthmoving equipment, we had got another to transport steelwork to a site up near Four Corners. That lasted a few months, and I was only involved in driving the escort vehicle up there a couple of times, as mostly I stayed in the workshop. Opportunities started to wind down after that contract, and things got quite sticky.

Jim acquired a couple of jobs to price, with which he asked me to help him. The first was for about $3,000, but the second was something like $25,000. I was very good friends with Jim, whose workshop it had been in the first place, and I didn't know whether Ron had just rented the space from him or bought it outright. As Trans Global was getting quiet, I thought it would be good for me to work with Jim on these jobs instead, which were nothing to do with trucking but instead engineering and steel work. Out at Jim's house, he had a lot of land and a big garage which we could use as a base. By now, Ron had a new lady friend called Sharon. She was a very nice woman and had taken over as manageress of the apartments. I wasn't included in the business side of Trans Global; that was all down to Ron. It seemed that we had too much outlay with all the extra trailers and drivers he required, and things were all starting to unravel. Finally, the bank pulled the plug on the company and it went bust.

By the way, both jobs had been accepted, but for whatever reason they never came off. That was one of the factors that made me want to leave. I was housesitting for my friend on the other side of Phoenix at the time, making sure he didn't get burgled while he was away on holiday, and I was taking Pooch to work with me each day at the workshop.

When July came around, it was time for me to go and meet Shirley, as we had arranged that she would come out to the States to visit me for three months during the school summer holidays (as a teacher, she had a lengthy break from work then). I asked Tom to come with me to the airport, and

I was grateful for his company, because I was nervous to say the least.

Meeting Shirley again was the best thing that had happened to me in a long while. Of course, she wasn't nervous like me; she was excited. She had never been to America before. The first thing I asked her as we neared the house was, "I hope you like dogs?" I had never mentioned Pooch to her before, but of course she loved dogs and fell in love with him immediately. We had a great time and started travelling around together. One of the first visits we made was to a crazy golf course. This place was about half the size of the Pleasure Beach in Blackpool. It was massive! Everything was full size, including big castles, mines, haunted houses, you name it. We had a super time until a skunk showed up and stunk the place out!

Shirley and I travelled all over Arizona, including to the edge of the Grand Canyon, to Flagstaff and to a ghost town called Jerome. It had been a mining town in the late 1800s but was now occupied by drop-outs and hippies making crafts to sell to tourists. We also went to Winslow, as mentioned in The Eagles song Take It Easy. The lyrics go, 'Standing on the corner in Winslow, Arizona'. Well, we stood on a corner, but probably not the right one – who cares!

One time, we were on a narrow mountain road when I spotted a massive tarantula walking along at the side of the road. I pulled in and got out with my camera. As I was quietly walking up to it, a car came around the corner and squashed it! This guy probably either didn't like spiders or thought he was saving my life. I thought it would make a great photograph, and he could have gone around it easily – the swine!

We also went to Sedona, where we went to a beautiful

church built into the rocks. It was called the Chapel of the Holy Cross. We lit a couple of candles: one for Shirley's dad and another for her uncle. Her uncle had recently died and left her some money. This had enabled Shirley to buy her plane ticket out to America. What a beautiful place the church was – so peaceful. We saw Montezuma's Castle, which is one of the very old cliff-dwelling places, and we found Montezuma Well in part of the Mogollon Rim, which is an escarpment that stretches about 200mi. In local folklore, there is supposedly a Mogollon monster, a creature seen as early as 1903 and spotted by one person a number of times between 1982 and 2004. It doesn't seem to be related to Big Foot, but it didn't put in an appearance for us anyway! The Petrified Forest was a weird place where the trees had turned to stone, and we saw staged shoot-outs in a couple of Western towns.

When my friends came back from their holiday, I had to move back into the apartments, and Shirley became good friends with Ron's girlfriend, Sharon. Shirley also gave Pooch a close haircut of his curly coat. She thought he looked good, but I remember thinking I had better not let her loose with those scissors on me! Nowadays, you'd call Pooch a cockapoo, but back in 1983 you'd never heard of any such thing.

The day after Ron's divorce from Paulette came through, he married Sharon. By then, Damien, Ron's son, had arrived. Believe you me, the wedding was nothing like you could imagine. Sharon wore a blouse and a skirt; Ron wore a shirt and pants. As we were getting ready to leave, Shirley was worried that she didn't have a suitable dress to wear to a wedding. She settled for the only proper dress she had, and I told her not to worry about it. The ceremony was held in what was just a small room adjacent to a hotel and a bar. The vicar wore a T-shirt, jeans and trainers and had just put some kind of robe around himself. It was just Ron and Sharon, the vicar and Shirley and me as witnesses. After the ceremony, we went into the bar next door to celebrate. The vicar took his robe off, came with us into the bar, then headed over to the nearest one-armed bandit and gambled away the money Ron had just paid him! I think this was Ron's fourth or fifth wedding, and now I can understand why.

After three months, it was coming to the end of Shirley's holiday, and I realised that my future belonged with her. I booked the same flight with her and said my goodbyes to everyone I knew. I was sorry to leave Tom, as we had become really good friends. He was also involved in the Vietnam War; what a super guy he was. By now, he was back working in the grinding trade with a new company and had moved to a really nice apartment block with a massive pool and hot tub. It was a gated complex that was locked at night. I took Shirley with me when I went to say farewell to Big John, which was another sad affair. We had gone through quite a bit together. The main question was what to do with our lovely dog, Pooch. We both loved him and had grown up with dogs. The quarantine law was for six months back then, and we both realised that this would be terrible for him, especially for a dog already so paranoid. We pondered on this for a while, and I didn't think Ron would be bothered looking after a dog, so I approached one of our ex-drivers. He and his wife had settled in Phoenix and were both now in their 60s. They were happy to have Pooch, and the dog would be company for the driver's wife while he was away trucking. All parties were happy with the outcome, and, although I was sorry to leave Pooch, I knew that he would have a good home.

When Shirley and I got back to England, we got ourselves a house. After 18 months, I wrote a letter to Tom telling him about our marriage. In his reply, he mentioned that Ron had started his own repair shop for wagon starter motors, dynamos and alternators. He was a clever bloke, so he could do anything like that. Tom told me that Ron was doing well and was happy with his life, as was Tom himself. I think Tom then moved out of those apartments, and I never got a forwarding address or telephone number for him.

Shirley and I went on to have three children, all boys. Our eldest son is Ryan, who is now 33 (born 2nd January 1987), then we have Aaron, who is 29 (born 19th May 1991), and then Brandon, who is 27 (born 9th April 1993). Aaron's partner, Becky, has a daughter called Renée who is seven years old.

I would love to chat with Tom, Ron and John now, as we would have 35 years to catch up on, talking about how life has treated us and reminiscing over the years we spent together. Now with technology so advanced it might be possible. Also, I would probably send them a copy of this book to let them know of the misadventures that life can throw at you – well it did for me!

The cabin on Ron's land, 1981. We look like the Beverly Hillbillies! I'm in the centre with Paulette, next row is Robert holding Paulette's daughter, Jerry, then Ron with his son. I can't remember the guy on the left's name

Gilligan's Butte, Ron's land, where we would chop down trees to sell; here is Ron with the mules, 1981

The salmon that Robert shot on the way up to Gilligan's Butte; it weighed 30lb

Me visiting Crater Lake, Oregon, 1981

The apartment in Phoenix where I stayed, 1982

My friends Big Ron and Tom at a party at the apartments

Me and the old Mack truck with one of the big wide loads

The workshop that we took over from Jim on the outskirts of Phoenix

Tom on the phone sourcing jobs for the truckers

Here is Shirley at the entrance of the biggest crazy golf course you can imagine, 1983

The Chapel of the Holy Cross, 1983

Montezuma Castle, 1983

Pooch, 1983

Ron and Sharon's wedding reception, August 1983

CONCLUSION
Written by Shirley

This is September 2020, and Pete has finished writing about his adventures. This year has been a very worrying time for everybody in the world. A horrible virus, COVID-19, has attacked the people, taking thousands of lives and changing the way we live. This made Pete question his mortality and realise he had better get his escapades down on paper just in case. As lockdown started in March 2020, Pete began to write and write and write every day for most of the day. I am so very proud of his achievements. As he was coming to the end, I realised that the hard work he had put in deserved to be saved, not just on paper, which could easily be torn, lost or crumpled, but instead put into a proper book.

We have been happily married for 35 years, and during this time Pete has told me lots of the adventures recorded in this book. There have been times when I have thought, gosh, life with us must be rather mundane after all his experiences! But I don't think he's ever had any regrets. We have three wonderful children, Ryan, Aaron and Brandon, and Pete is very proud of them. He has always been involved in their activities, achievements and adventures. We hope that in time their children, grandchildren and great-grandchildren will enjoy reading Pete's escapades and will have their own adventures, be surrounded with love and lead happy, fulfilled lives.

With love to you all, Shirley and Pete.

FAMILY
ALL BECAUSE TWO PEOPLE FELL IN LOVE

Shirley and me with our children, Ryan, Aaron and Brandon

Printed in Great Britain
by Amazon